A Year In E

The Fauna And Flora Of A Norfolk Estate

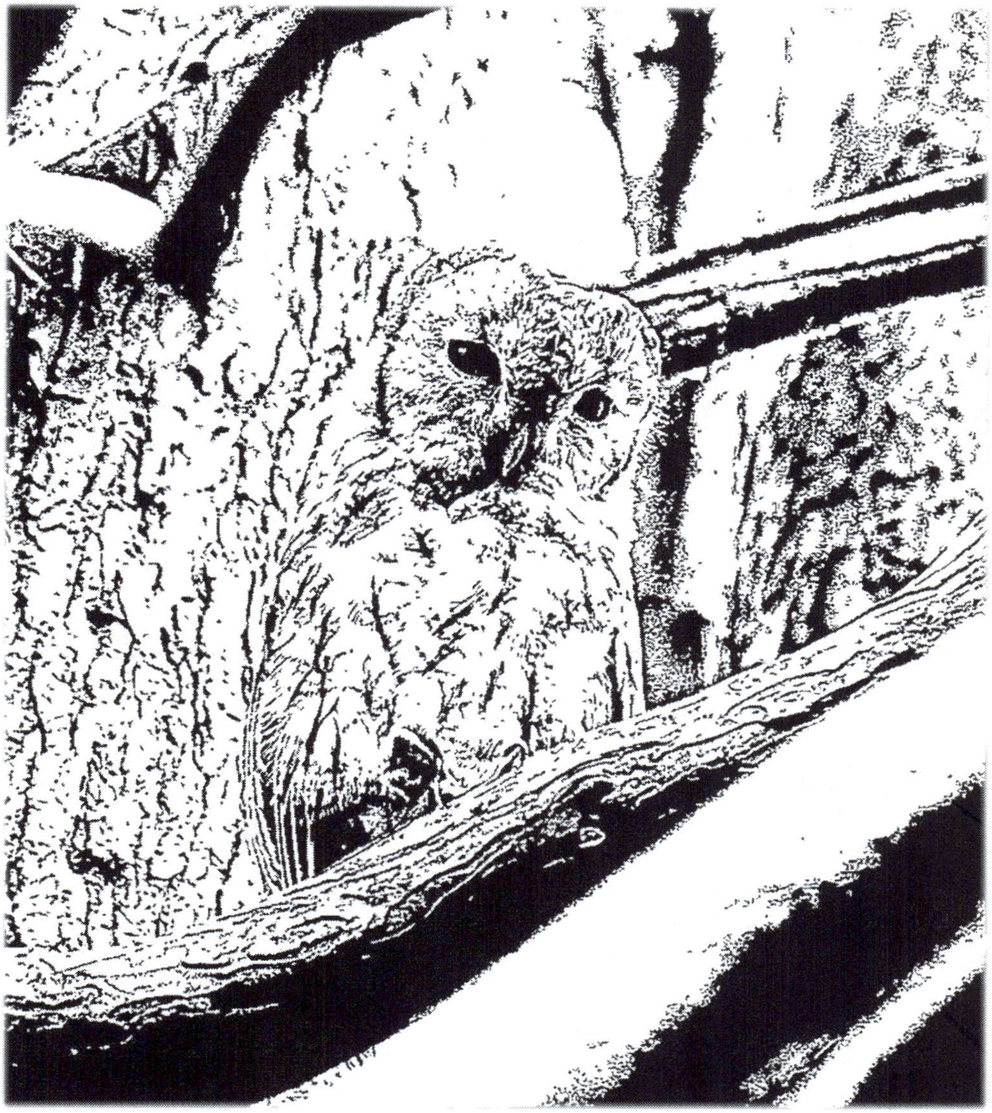

Ian Barnett

To Chantelle Enjoy the read!

I.

- NOV.16

Preface

Do you have an 'Eden'? A special place, a wilderness where you go to escape modern life's hustle and bustle. I have the privilege of such a sanctuary. Eden, of course, is not its real name. It is a very private place. A thousand acres of woodland, hedgerow, river, wild meadow, pasture and crops. Deep in the heart of Norfolk. In return for the privilege of walking there, my contribution is to help keep down the small vermin on the estate. The usual suspects … rat, rabbit, grey squirrel, stoat, woodpigeon and corvid. Yet this book is rarely about that. This is not a managed, commercial shooting estate, though the wild game is encouraged to stay with a few feeders. This is purely for a couple of 'family and friend' shoots each season. Thus, as there is no full time gamekeeper, my humble efforts are welcomed. My 'Eden' sits across an escarpment above a tranquil, snaking chalk-stream river. One of the longest in Norfolk. Home to trout, barbel, dace, pike and chub. Along the river margins, otters thrive and mink menace. Despite this, I've found water vole sign often. Flora and fauna are abundant. The varied landscape is perfect for raptors and many of their species breed here. Buzzard, sparrowhawk, kestrel, barn owl, tawny owl and little owl are regularly seen. Almost every land-borne British mammal exists here or has passed through during the years I have enjoyed walking this small corner of England. Red, roe, muntjac and fallow deer … but (not yet) Chinese water deer or sika. Weasel, stoat, rat, rabbit, hare, field mouse, wood mouse, common shrew, bank vole are here. Grey squirrels (my main reason for being allowed here) drove out the native reds (that held out so long in Norfolk) many years before I came here. The owner and tenant farmers on the estate allow me to walk freely with gun, dog and camera. For that I am forever indebted. This book, quite simply, is a celebration of a typical year in my own, personal 'Eden'.

Topography

*"So on he fares, and to the border comes
Of Eden, where delicious Paradise,
Now nearer, crowns with her enclosure green"*

(Paradise Lost, Book IV - John Milton, 1608-1674)

Eden ... some reference points for the reader.

Dedication

This book is dedicated to Lady Ann Prince-Smith, who so kindly allows me the freedom of her huge garden. To own Eden is a huge responsibility. To permit me access to Eden is a quantum leap in trust that I can never under-estimate. I hope this record of the fauna and flora that populate this wonderful place will in some way recompense that trust.

Legal Stuff

All rights to this work are reserved. No part of this publication may be reproduced, stored in or by any means (mechanical, electrical, photocopying, recording or otherwise) without the prior written permission of the publisher, who is the author. Any person who does any unauthorised act in relation to this publication may be liable to criminal prosecution and civil claims for damages.

The right of Ian Barnett to be identified as the author of this work has been asserted by him in accordance with the Copyright, Designs and Patents Act 1988.

All text and photo-illustrations in this work were supplied by the author and remain his copyright.

Copyright © Ian Barnett 2016

January

This is the real 'bleak mid-winter' for me, yet a time when I can re-coup and prepare for the coming year. We all need a 'cycle', otherwise life can become relentless. The post-Christmas period is a time for the hunter, writer and naturalist (for I am all) to set some aspirations for the months ahead. What do I want to achieve, what would I like to photograph, what books and articles are planned? A New Year, new opportunities and new challenges. I have stayed away from the coverts over the Yuletide period, to allow the family guns their Boxing Day sport undisturbed. On Eden, little will have changed. In my experience, there will be nearly as many wild pheasants left now as there were on the opening day of the season. Unlike farm-reared poults, bought in from a dealer, these wild birds are canny and wood-wise.

At dawn, a barn owl sits on a fence-post along the edge of the old orchard, watching me intently. I dare not move, frozen in admiration. Its brown mottled wings, white breast and moon-like face captivate me. Unblinking, its head dips and rises occasionally in an almost hypnotic motion. The weather, so far, has been kind to the vole hunter. The moment is broken as it slips off the fence, soundlessly, to float over the lea like a giant moth. I keep my vigil, enjoying the sight of such a skilled hunter at work. The owl suddenly hovers momentarily before plunging headlong, talons stretched, into the dew-sodden tussocks. After a few seconds the owl labours upwards, something furry in its grip, before dropping again into the sodden grass. *Tyto alba* takes his breakfast in private.

Snow flurries as I finish work! My heart leaps as I study the pregnant clouds. The forecast is good; or bad? Depending on whether you like snow or not. I certainly do. Later I walk the lurcher in the dark and the soft fat white flakes settle on my bob-cap and his coat. I retire to bed with the expectation of a child on Christmas Eve. I will be walking Eden and its virgin snowfields tomorrow.

The Meadow Witch lopes across the snow-scape looking rudely healthy. An ice queen. An extra from a Disney film, her wide eyes twinkling with reflected crystal. I expect to see a dappled deer kid emerge onto the margin followed by his majestic, antlered sire. Instead, I see a fox watching from the woods edge. He is in full winter coat and looks as fit as a rufus flea. He won't waste his energy on a fruitless hare-course. The Witch has the snow-field to herself.

The mercury has fallen so low, the small pond in Garden Wood has frozen over. The cattle huddle by the dyke beside the wood, thwarted from total sanctuary by the deep water. The flat cattle pasture and water meadows are devoid of cover and unforgiving to beast and man. The icy Siberian blast cuts across them like an invisible tsunami. I pull my bob-cap down tight and pull my snood up, to cover my ears and cheeks. Out near the river, a harnser lifts and flaps its huge wings. An ice-age pterodactyl. I scour the frozen pastures but there are no sign of mammoths. Just the frosted-breath Friesians.

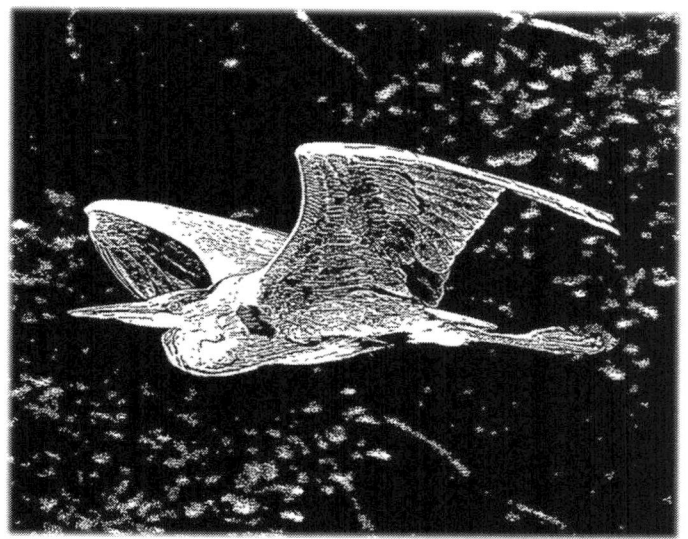

A stand of oak and beech line the edge of the winter wood. Devoid of leaf, the bare trees look like a guard of naked warriors. Spartans; arms raised against an unseen foe. Muscle and limb exposed for all to see; as are their scars ... the legacy of a myriad battles with gale, frost, squirrel and deer. The trees will spend their spring and summer taking on sustenance, growing and building strength. They will shelter, feed and house bird, beast and insect. The autumn and winter will test their resolve and their roots. I respect trees. Trees are the super-heroes of Mother Nature's endless story.

The gathering of the rooks out on the plough seems to have a purpose. The birds with the baggy trousers certainly aren't feeding though. They are noisy and quarrelsome. Two or three birds, in the centre of the melee, being seemingly harangued by the others. These rook 'parliaments' are much recorded in country lore. I have never seen the 'kangaroo-court' type attacks and killing during such an event which others claim to have seen. It all looks like petty squabbling and scrimmaging to me. Did one covet another's mate? Did it steal a twig from a neighbours nest or hi-jack another rook's plump leather-jacket? The rooks know; we can only speculate.

I heard a misinformed young radio presenter on our local station mention that squirrels are hibernating at the moment. This caused immediate concern, as I was on my way to the estate to cull a few more brush-tails while the leaf cover is sparse. I hated to think that I might disturb their slumber! I needn't have worried, though. My greys must have set their alarm clocks, bless them. Despite the cold, there were plenty foraging for food. When I left, I pondered whether I should take my sack of squirrels to the radio station, to explain that these specimens were now in a permanent state of hibernation. I despair at the sort of education are we giving our youth? Squirrels don't hibernate. They will curl up in the warmth and dry of the drey in the most inclement weather but they will always come out daily to feed.

Along the North drive, the winter die-back has revealed a stone seat and sun-dial amongst the naked shrubbery. I scribble down the epithets engraved on three of its four sides so that I can translate them later. The one on the fourth side, I'm able to interpret. *'Amyddst ye flowres I tell ye houres'*. In Shakespeare's time they clearly didn't do 'spell-check'. The shadow on the sun-dial tells me the sun is falling. I move on. At home, I use the power of the mighty oracle (Google) to translate the words on the sundial. *'Vide et vade'* appears to be Latin for 'Take a look'. That makes sense. So too does *'Rein sans le soleil'* which is French for 'Nothing without the sun'. The sun-dial is, after all, like the solar panel in that respect. Useless. The last one intrigues me. *'Tak' tent o' time ere time be tint'*. A popular Scottish platitude, apparently. 'Take account of time, lest time runs out'. Wise words indeed.

A freeze has descended upon the land, the overnight breath of some Arctic god. The rooks drift across the frost-capped furrows like black chevrons; caricature birds scribbled on a Lowry canvas. The leather-jacket and the worm are locked deep beneath the frozen soil. The rooks are hungry. Everything is hungry. Nature's larder is on lockdown.

I take a slow drive up the concrete track towards the Hall and scrutinise the rides to my right. There is no sign of squirrel, rabbit or magpie. A carrion crow lifts from some sort of mischief within the beech grove and sweeps out onto the plough. I follow its flight with my eyes, which quickly pick up an aberration. I'm close to a telegraph pole and something large is sitting on top. I slide the DSLR from the passenger seat and turn it on, extending the zoom lens. The buzzard poses beautifully. The estates 'grandfather', over-wintering as always. A predator carefully surveying his hunting domain; just as I am.

Out near the hoar-frosted water meadows, a pair of rum looking waterfowl sweep past, honking noisily. They look, for all the world, like a pair of pugilists who have been on the equal side of a brutally hard fight. The dark rings around the eyes are deceptive. They are Egyptian geese or 'Gyppos' as the local wild-fowlers call them. The pair will stay together for life, as long as Nature permits.

Sitting along the woods flank, the dog and I watch the progress of the plough as it turns out deep furrows behind the tractor. Regimental lines etched accurately by some distant satellite; an eye in the sky steering a land-locked machine. The gulls and rooks don't care how straight the trenches are; only how many worms and leatherjackets are exposed in the process.

The kestrel looks famished on this bitter morning. He is keeping vigil on a bare branch, surveying his frosted territory. Most of his prey are pegged beneath a hoary grass-scape that glitters in the weak winter sun. Just one glimpse of movement, just a single vole strike, will help him survive another day.

The shooting season is all but done yet still the foolish pheasant cocks face-off and fight. Don't they realise they have just survived to live at least another nine months?

February

February, to me, is the nadir of winter; the most barren month in the calendar. The land has been scoured by frost, ice, rain and gale. The trees still stand naked and stark. Both bird and beast struggle to find sustenance. Though global warming and the shift of 'El Nino' produce milder winters, February is still the sparsest time. Siberian winds cut across the river valley from the East to whip the escarpment. They slap the rose-cheeked face and nip at ears and fingers. These are the weeks when I, just like the deer and hare, seek solace in the twelve-acre wood with its West-facing slopes and conifers. Days for hats and gloves; hand-warmers and hot soup. Though the flora and fauna struggle, Eden is still very much alive. February is also the month of the snowdrop. Down in the garden wood, there is an avalanche.

Motoring up the concrete track towards the farm, a plump and gaudy pheasant sits atop some plastic wrapped silage bales. Cock o' the manor. I smile to myself and salute him as I pass. I had already heard that the wind and rain made for a poor final-day shoot. He and many others have survived to see another season. With hens aplenty, I would have some purpose patrolling the hedge bottoms and beetle banks this spring and summer. These birds have more than just Reynard to worry about. There are smaller vermin which are just as threatening to egg, poult and adult. Rats, grey squirrels, carrion crows, stoats and magpies all predate ground nesting species. Not just the pheasants and partridges but also the larks, buntings, warblers, woodcock, lapwings and others.

Early February is the bleakest time in my Norfolk calendar. A time that sours the taste in the mouth of both naturalist and shooter. Winters die-back is complete. Apart from the evergreens, all other vegetation has retreated. The holly, ivy, mistletoe, yew, box and some conifers hold court against the dark, skeletal landscape of barren wood and hedge. The only sound today is from the ivy-curtain where I crouch in pursuit of roosting pigeons. The tedious *"drip, drip, drip"* of fog-born moisture. Behind the thin, grey curtain is a semblance ... a mere hint ... of a low winter sun. It feels no need to force through, however. There are few living things needing its solace? There are few living things needing solace because the low winter sun has failed to force through! A foolish sun on a forlorn day in a foul, foetid month.

There are small flocks of Canada geese on the water meadows which I can't see for the fog. I can hear them honking though and occasionally a pair will break through the mist and beat heavily across the escarpment.

You know the weather is at its harshest when the grey squirrel tables, the flat pine stumps, show stripped pine cones. Long gone is the nutritious protein of the cob nut and acorn. The pine cone is the squirrels 'silage'; the winter fall-back fruit.

🍃

The ducks cheer me up when the weather is bad. I'm not a wildfowler but I love the whistle of the wigeon as they flight in to the water meadow splashes at dusk. The fowl seem love the harsh weather and celebrate it with their haunting calls and their congregational flying displays.

🍃

The dullness of each dreary day seeps into the soul like a demonic possession. For me, the lack of sunlight nibbles at my psyche and I seek relief, writing indoors under the glare of an S.A.D. light. Does it read as though it has done me any good? No ... I thought not. I put down my pen, pull on my boots and head for Eden. Better drowned in a fog-swamped fugue than falling from the ceiling, having climbed up the walls to get there. If I can't get sunlight, at least I can feel the bitter breeze on my face and simply feel alive. Just to climb the slippery escarpment and make the heart race clears the lungs and invigorates the soul again.

In the birthing enclosure, with its straw beds and slush, the cows are in parturition. There are several healthy newcomers already. It seems, to me, a harsh time to be born ... but what do I know? Up on the cattle-shed roof the magpies and crows are gathering. Each new calving brings fast food. The after-births are full of nutrition for the winter corvid.

The peacocks on Eden are the watchdogs and guardians of the Old Hall. There is little that escapes their attention and they are also intelligent enough to recognise the regular visitors that bear no malice. Turn up in a strange vehicle and they will announce you raucously. Even my old lurcher, trained to ignore them, can pass close to the birds with me without even the rustle of a feather. We are privileged in having earned a free pass from the vividly coloured sentinels.

The die-back is complete; only the evergreens hold any leaf. The squirrel dreys are exposed so it's a good time to watch them. Grey squirrels build seasonal dreys. A spring and summer residence in the outer boughs to enjoy the breeze and sun. The winter drey will be close to the trunk, often in ivy or a cleft of thick branches to maximise shelter and heat retention.

After misery, there is always joy. The snowdrops and winter aconites have sprung forth to lay a carpet of renewal and expectation across the floor of the Garden Wood. If the wood is a paragraph, this is its punctuation. I love this place at this time. A doe appears from her hideout in a cluster of wild box. She tests the air, upwind of my cover. The lurcher stands next to me, watching her too. The deer stares at us but can't see us. I look like a stand of vegetation in my clothing; the dog looks like a clump of snowdrops. The doe is unconvinced, it seems. Her nose twitches again and catches our scent. Her departure is as swift as the flick of the lurchers tail.

Turning into the entrance to the Hall, at the far end of the drive, the rear end of my motor keeps travelling instead of straightening up. Suddenly I'm facing in the direction I came from? Black ice. Oh well, no damage done, except to my pride. I look around the open fields and into the farmyard. I don't think anyone saw it … did they?

He flashes past, along the newly turned furrows below the escarpment. He looks in better health than last month as he turns and sweeps back along the dead nettle margins. The windhover lights on a branch to study the sparse undergrowth below. He is faring better now and will survive the winter.

A tiny muntjac doe creeps from beneath the junipers to stand in the snow, staring at me with what looks like a plea for help. She is trembling, probably frozen. There is nothing I can do for her. She will either survive or fall, for that is Natures way.

Virgin snow is heaven for me. I kit myself in layers; mitts, merino socks, boots, fleece knickers and a bob hat. The cold won't be allowed to interfere with the opportunity to track and trail; to understand what fauna walks the estate when I can't see them.

Outside one of the sheds near the farm, an ancient anvil lies abandoned and rusting. On this bitterly cold morning I stand staring at it, imagining the industry it has seen. I can hear the clang and crash of the smithy's hammer, shaping molten red iron. I can smell the scent of searing, smoking hoof and imagine the crimson glow from the brazier. Oh for that searing brazier right now, as my breath hangs around me like a wraith in the freezing air!

I love crows. Their affinity with my Norfolk landscape is undeniable. *Corvidae*. An iconic avian family. Mischief makers, predators, knaves and thieves. As infamous as pirates yet just as loved. Clever and cunning. Opportunistic and adaptable. They say that after the Apocalypse, rats will rule the earth? I'd put my money on the crows.

I hate crows. They have no respect for any other species. Bandits and robbers. Egg plunderers and chick murderers. They use their lofty pinnacles to spy and plot their crimes. They shout my presence to all other creatures within a miles radius. *"Guuun! Guuun! Guuuun!"* Their affinity with killing fields is legendary. Plucking the eyeballs from the fallen corpse and feasting on entrails. The devils birds.

Down in the garden wood, I rub my eyes in disbelief. Did I have one glass too much last night? The leaf mulch is moving! On closer inspection I find that it's a procession of common toads. They are making their way from the shrubbery around the Hall to the big pond, to breed.

A honking skein of greylag geese appears out of the freezing morning fog. So low, I can feel the down-draught from their wings as they pass overhead. They alight in the adjoining water meadow. A magnificent and noisy communal crash-landing that wakes the whole valley.

A kaleidoscope of black and white confuses the eye out on the meadow. What looks like an avian game of 'tag' as the pied crows chase and cackle. A pillage of magpies. Is their winter flocking merely just safety in numbers? Is it a tribal unification? One thing is for certain, it is also about 'genetics'. The combinations of families that winter together give way to the pairing-off of the youngsters. New territories are forged and the gene pool is kept fresh, minimising in-breeding. Undoubtedly why these pied pirates have multiplied so successfully over the past twenty years. I have my own version of the old nursery rhyme about magpies. May I share it?

One for sorrow, two for joy
Three for a girl, four for a boy
Five for a rabble, six for a pack
Seven for a pillage, eight, an attack
Nine for a plunder, ten for a fury
Eleven for a murder, twelve for the jury.

A foggy, murky morning and the water meadows seem to have adopted a host of melted snowmen overnight. Either that … or the gods have cast three-score pillows across the sodden turf? I wipe my fogged glasses. The mute swans are gathering. The winter colonies are large. I would guess that, as well as safety in numbers, they flock to socialise before the youngsters' pair off and mate. I lean on the field gate and watch the new arrivals coming in. The percussions, the heavy down-draught from the swan's huge wingspan, boom through the moist morning air. The incoming cobs and pens glide into sight through the mist. Their landings are awkward and ugly as they hit the pools. On the water, the swan is serene. In the air? They only just wing it.

My 'raison d'etre' on Eden is small vermin control. Not least that little imp, the grey squirrel. Don't be fooled by its cute appearance. It is an egg and chick raider *par excellence*. Agile, cunning, intelligent and adaptive it makes for a formidable foe. It also damages both saplings and mature trees with its habit of bark-stripping. Its fecundity makes it nigh impossible to eradicate, every cleared acre being repopulated within weeks; for Nature abhors a vacuum and *Sciurus carolinensis* certainly knows how to fill a void.

The deep troughs below the winter potato plough hold secrets, if you search for them. Today a covey of Frenchmen are hiding in the trenches. *Alectons rufa*. As they scurry along the channels, the partridges disturb another rut-dweller ... a brown hare. Soil and stone scatters behind him as Lepus engages sixth gear and disappears across the nearby stubbles. It's disheartening watching an Englishman run from Frenchmen but in truth, he was running from me. Such is Natures warning system. It has a 'ripple' effect. The hare was spooked because the birds were spooked by me.

Stepping down the slope from the pine wood, I near the copse at the bottom. Glancing left into the sugar beet crop I witness a pair of roe deer 'in flagrante delicto'. A stout looking buck is covering a doe. Not a sight to linger on, but rare nonetheless. I take a pornographic picture for my archives and creep away, a stalking voyeur.

In the middle of the Garden Wood there is a pit. A small dell. Its history and former purpose unknown to me. Surrounded now by yew, box, azalea and rhododendron it is the ultimate spot for any wild creature (including me) trying to find sanctuary from winters icy blast or summers searing sun. It has its own micro-climate, temperate all year round. Today, a bitter February morning, I step quietly to the lip of the dell and look down into the murk of the hollow. At first, I see nothing. Then my eyes adjust to the gloom. A hare rises first, scenting my intrusion. Then a muntjac appears from nowhere, sniffing the air before creeping away. A grey squirrel spits in anger, above me. A trio of hen pheasants, survivors of the season, scuttle for the cover of the shrubbery. The squirrel hisses again and pays the price for its inhospitality. I squat for a while and take on some hot soup. I feel a tad guilty. My own need for shelter has brought disturbance and death. That the squirrel felt threatened is understandable. Their control is my main role here. To the other creatures, I should be simply benign.

In the storage pad on the farm, the sugar beet tubers are piled high awaiting the trucks. Soon, a fleet of eight-wheelers will cart the crop to Cantley for processing. The lanes of Norfolk will be clogged with the lorries as long as the sugar campaign continues.

In the stark winter wood I decide to take a tour with the camera instead of the gun. The jays on Eden persistently evade my attention when I have a rifle in my hands. Today, they embarrass me with their flagrant posing and posturing.

She can't even see me, so focussed is her hunger. A vixen prowls towards me across the hoar-hardened stubble. Her eyes, her whole demeanour, express desperation. Like me she has just seen the Meadow Witch lope into cover. Looking at the vixen's condition, my money is on the Witch.

March

Perhaps it's the Welsh ancestry running through my blood that makes me smile when the first daffodils bloom. There are plenty here on Eden. Not just along the North Drive, where they revive every spring but also randomly across the whole estate. They look strangely out of place in the wild corners; almost lonely.

The snowdrops are wilting now but the yellow winter aconites sprinkle the woodland floor. It's as though the world has turned upside down; the stars are on the mulchy morning carpet instead of hanging high in the evening sky.

The slough of my soaking boots through the sodden grass is rewarded by a view of hares on the deep potato plough. This estate is blessed with them. There are three chasing and boxing; skipping over the cloying marl like ballet dancers. The legendary March madness is upon them. The fighting is mere 'handbags at dawn'. Contrary to popular belief the fisticuffs isn't between male hares fighting for the privilege of covering the fair maiden. The boxer is the female, doing what females of most species do … teasing and playing hard to get, despite the urge to procreate. She will make her choice soon. There will be leverets again on the hillside this Spring for the buzzard to test.

There is a 'windhover' over the orchard meadow. The grass there is reasonably long and rarely touched by a blade. A haven for voles and mice. The kestrel needs killing grounds like this in the winter or he would starve. Every farm and estate should have wild meadows like this. They are a lifeline for the conservation of small mammals and raptors. The barn owl hunts here, too, at twilight and dawn.

Sitting on a post in the cow pasture, *Athena noctua* sits stoically, watching the world go by. My favourite bird of all; the little owl. Why do I bond with the little owl so much? Because it is a small, observant and skilful hunter. It feeds on the small stuff. Like me.

The field below the escarpment has been sown and a rare seen visitor is feasting on the seed. Sometimes heard singing on high just before a summer storm the mistle thrush, *Turdus viscivorus*, takes it fill and steals away.

Watching the magpie pair building their nest brings a crisis of conscience. They journey from woodland floor to pine crest a thousand times a day with broken twigs. Their industry is immense and their construction skill, enigmatic. This is their first nest, this first year mating. So using skills inherited. Genetic. No bird could teach another such intricacy. That interwoven dome; a fortress with a single entrance. A labour of necessity and natural wonder. Yet I cannot let the pair endure. Hence the moral dilemna. From their keep they will watch every songbird build their nest and brood. They will see every game-birds scrape and know where the eggs are for the taking. I need to put conscience aside and ensure the safety and survival of the majority. So I do.

There are Frenchmen in the cattle pasture. Just a few, scuttling along comically, heads bobbing above the grass. Red-legged partridges. Je les aime!

A black sentinel balances on the pinnacle sprigs of a wind blown spruce. From his lofty perch, the carrion crow is surveying his territory while his mate sits on eggs nearby. *Corvus corone* is an early breeder, building its nest in the leafless tree before many lesser birds have even mated. He sits now observing all the prey birds constructing their puny, slender nests. His intelligence and cunning will be mentally mapping where to find eggs and chicks as the breeding season develops. He has an eye on everything ... and I have a very close eye on him.

Crouched behind an ivy break at the edge of the wood I pull my snood against the icy breeze. I'm waiting for the flick of a long ear or the hint of grey / brown fur within the briars. Just one coney will do, if they brave the chill to feed. Further along the fence line I glimpse a patch of rufus fur. A vixen, stalking low to the ground, cat-style. She is moving away, like me using the breeze in her favour. She looks in poor health, exhausted and half starved. I deduce that she is feeding cubs and that there must be a nursery den nearby. I withdraw stealthily. Her need is greater than mine so I leave the meagre warren to her and her alone.

Returning to the car on a bitterly cold afternoon, the dying sun silhouettes one of the guardians of the gates. If I was asked to 'market' Eden, this would be its logo. A bird of paradise.

Above the water meadow, two birds are engaged in what first resembles a conflict. One pursues the other as they wheel, climb, plummet, twist and glide. They fly in tandem, never touching. Each jink and turn expertly executed. A magical aerial ballet; the dancers dressed in a dark, iridescent green and pure white. Their paddle shaped wings and plaintive call identify the duo. *"Peewit, peewit"*. Lapwings at their courtship display. A common sight in my distant youth, everywhere. Alas now, a spectacle to behold and hold close in your memory before it disappears for ever. Such is the decline of this beautiful bird, sadly accelerated by the general publics naïve support for the fox and the badger. Lapwings are ground nesting birds. What hope do such birds have against the nocturnal scouring of Brock and Reynard?

A broad billed bird trills amid the shrubbery, close to the Hall. A common sight in the hedgerows of my youth, it has become less common in rural areas now. The elegant chorister in his fern green jacket is now more commonly seen in the urban garden; at the bird table. It is a male greenfinch and my day is all the better for both seeing him and hearing his song.

I'm tucked behind some scrub in the garden wood and glimpse a hint of rufus fur through the foliage. I pull the dog in tight beside me. The camera is readied and I use the tiny hen-squeaker on my key ring to imitate a dying rabbit. In he comes, drawn by the irresistible sound of an easy meal. The breeze doesn't favour us and at about twenty yards, he hesitates. Standing behind a tree trunk he sniffs the air and fluffs up his brush in alarm. Soon he is gone, having taken our scent. A handsome dog fox ... but best he keeps away from the peacocks!

April

The tumble of brown fur catches my eye and I stoop to hide behind a decomposing bale. I pull a camera from my bag. There are new souls to steal. A litter of fox-cubs, six in all, playing at the corner of the covert. Probably their first excursion from the nursery den, exploring this exciting world in the warm spring sunshine. I enjoy a magical half-an-hour of entertainment as the cubs cavort and scent and mock-fight. I get too close and a couple spot me; too green to sense peril, they sit and stare at me curiously. Then a sharp *'yap'* within the copse destroys the moment. The cubs obey the unseen mother and withdraw to the den.

Before the hedgerow growth erupts in full, I make a tour of the estate perimeter. A three mile reconnaissance mission with no other purpose but curiosity. Like Old Charlie marking his territory, my boot-prints stake my claim. I stop short of depositing scats on hummock or stump. Nor do I cock a leg at every post around the land; I leave that to the lurcher. On my trek I see plenty to hold my interest. Badger latrines, barn owl pellets below gate-posts, clustered red deer hair on barbed wire; the bark of a rudely interrupted roebuck in the alder carr. The flight of two score woodpigeon from a previously unknown roost. The buzzard and his new lady follow my progress, mewing and soaring. Out on the thickly ploughed marl, a hare rises from its form to canter into cover. My Eden is marked out for another season, all changes mentally noted. Yet little, really, has changed.

The sound of a Gatling-gun disturbs the tranquillity of the morning. In the Escarpment Wood, a Great Spotted Woodpecker (*Dendrocopos major*) is either chiselling its nest hole or simply showing off. I chance too near, trying to grab sight of the handsome bird but it spots me and retreats with that harsh, repeated and scolding '*tchik*'. The Great Spotted and its habits are very different from the Green Woodpecker which I see here often too. The Green, *Picus viridis*, is more of a meadow feeder so often seen out on the sward. I often confuse its alarm call with the hunting chime of the sparrowhawk.

Hundreds of green caterpillars dangle precariously above my head as I crouch beneath a brookside spinney. They are cascades of hazel catkins. From these will fruit the winter cob nuts.

A pair of water-hens have nested on the fringe of the garden pond. Harmless little dabchicks which live on filtered pond life. Only a generation ago, moorhens would have been fair game for the table. Indeed, during the right season it is still legal though I can't ever imagine myself being hungry enough to shoot and pluck a moorhen. I like to see them slip into the water and paddle away, especially with a flotilla of chicks following them. Like the water vole, they are being decimated by mink ... yet ignored by conservationists?

Eden's rookery is a corner of the estate where I rarely venture, near the North lodge. I don't abide by the 'tradition' of shooting the branchers (the fledgling rooks) in May. Good training for a youngster trying to master the rifle or shotgun ... but hardly sport. I watch the busy rookery this morning. All bustle and industry as the rooks fly back and forth feeding the hatching chicks. I love rooks. They have a 'Britishness' about them.

There are two of us keeping a vigil in the twelve-acre wood on this spring morning. I'm busy watching a magpie nest but the bird that has just descended nearby is watching something else. His eyes are bright and alert. His head tilting now and again. While I wait for the thieves to return to their lair, the kestrel is watching for wood-mice on the forest margin.

All around the estate there are primroses in bloom; the yellow rosettes contrasting highly with verdant leaves. Their scent after an April shower is real marker that spring has arrived.

Another post-dawn barn owl moment as I stand on the escarpment above the Orchard Meadow. From my lofty viewpoint I watch her, a white owl, quartering the one acre field. Her flight is like bated breath, anti-sonic. Her slow, circular sweeps become more accentuated; concentrated. She knows her quarry is moving somewhere in the sub-sward. She halts, fanning her broad wings, then drops into the tall strangle of grasses. A second later she emerges gripping her prize then sweeps towards me and the wood. The long tail of her kill, as she soars past, tells me she has caught a field mouse. The owl glides through the wood and out of sight. Has she a brood already?

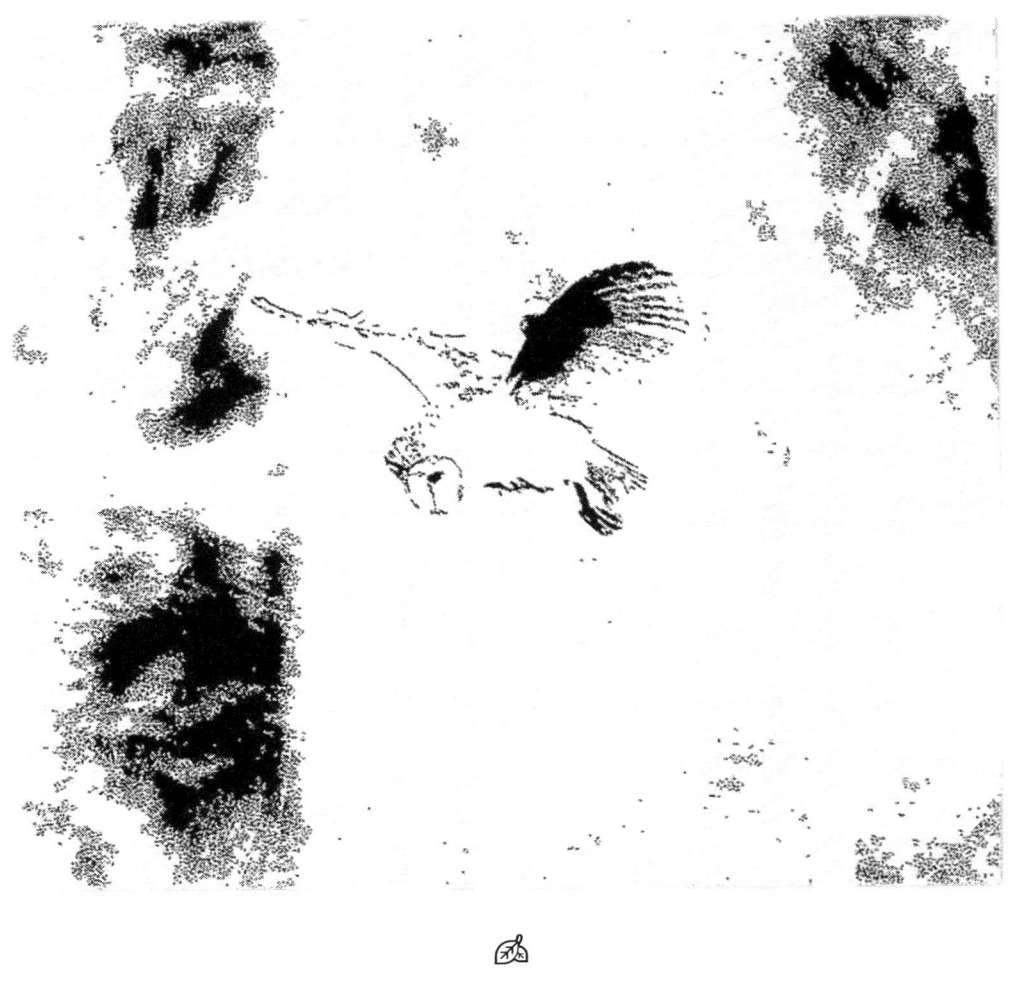

Clouds, shower, sunshine, clouds, shower, sunshine, clouds, shower, sunshine. Repeat ten more times and throw the odd rainbow into the sequence. It's April. I love April. Often four seasons in one day, which is perfect for the writer, photographer and hunter in me.

Another new sett has been excavated over in the pine wood. The whole of the hill here is undermined with deep burrows. The wood is turning into a sort of badger 'ghetto'. Sapling guards are scattered like matchsticks. The latrines are stinking and covered in flies (proving that badgers do, truly, shit on their own doorstep). Long trails run through the coverts, eroded by the shuffle of bristly underbelly.

Above the briars, a huge dragonfly zooms back and forth chasing the hoverflies collecting nectar on the flowers. A Southern Hawker; *Aeshna cyanea*.

All over the estate the cock blackbirds are scrapping like street urchins. It's the blackbird 'rut'. Hens are being courted and rival suitors chased across invisible boundaries. Nests will be built soon. Many folk ignore the blackbird; a victim of its own commonality. Serious fans of *Turdus merula* (like me) love the bird for its evensong ... such a celebration of another day survived. For me, they are also the woods earlier warning system. The harsh 'chink' when it sees fox, squirrel or rat. The shrill, hysterical scolding of the flying blackbird tells of direct and immediate threat such as man or sparrowhawk. That call has revealed the presence of many a poacher to the gamekeeper over the years.

Near the end of April I chance on a blackbirds nest, hidden in a tangle of dog-rose. Four pale blue eggs mottled in fairy scribble. The hen gave away her secret, panicked into flight as I passed the spot. Had she sat tight, I would never have known the nest was there. Will it survive predation? Only time will tell.

There are two distinctive hares on the estate whose paths cross mine often; the Meadow Witch and the Wood Witch. The former has shorter, black-tipped ears. If not for her size she could almost be mistaken for a rabbit. The latter, however, has ears to die for. Full-on Jodrell Bank radar dishes. She is a middle-aged matriarch, I am sure. Was she born in the wood and thus developed those large ears to cope with the challenges of a life amongst trees? I catch a glimpse of the Meadow Witch on the open sward near the Pine Wood. She is plump with young. There will indeed be a bevy of little sorcerers on the field this spring.

I once wrote, insanely, to look like a tree you need to think like a tree. What does a tree think, though? It thinks nothing. It just is. Standing innocuously in its place, arms thrown wide. It gives shelter, life, sap, fruit, sanctuary, sustenance and oxygen. In death it gives timber, firewood, pulp, charcoal ... or simply lies rotting. Nurturing insects and fungi. Going back, slowly, to the Tao. Returning its nitrates and goodness into the earth from whence it sprang, as a tiny shoot battling against weather and predation. Today, dressed from head to foot in camo, I consider this. I decide that I could never be so useful. So I take off my camouflage head-net and go home.

The cracks and crevices in the many mature yew, oak and willow trees around the estate play host to the several jackdaw colonies around the estate. My observation, year on year, has given me a metal map of where most are. I spend some time today just watching the behaviour of a pair who have chosen an old woodpecker hole for the third year running. Jakes (as we call them here) are very cautious and secretive around their nest site. Usually noted as a very vocal little crow, the jackdaw will do everything in its power to avoid advertising the location of the nest. While the female is sitting, the male is feeding her. He appears with food some distance from the hole and scouts around, checking for predators, before flying straight into the hole. When the chicks have hatch, both will behave the same way as they bring flies, beetles, grubs and even songbird chicks to the young.

The old lurcher emerges from a hedgerow ditch draped in a self-sticking camouflage. He turns crazy circles, snatching at the strands of weed with his teeth. I help him out, pulling the last of the suckers from his coat. The dog then starts to chew at the plant. It is 'cleavers' ... that self perpetuating tumbleweed that clings to fur and feather. The seeds are therefore widely distributed. Dogs, for some reason, find the sap from the stems irresistible. It seems to soothe their digestive system.

The old lodge at the end of the North drive has a very unusual chimney ... but with a familiar problem. I doubt that the flues are used any more, so the jackdaw nests are probably harmless?

Rare intruders catch my eagle eye today. Across the river valley, beyond river and road, there is a huge fallow herd. Some fifty strong. A small scouting party of fifteen have breached the natural defences. Yearling's and does. I shrink into the foliage and they pass by within fifty yards, nose to tail. Pausing at a barbed wire fence, they shuffle about as if unsure who should leap first but a couple catch my scent. The swift exodus, again nose to tail, is back the way they came. A delightful sight for the observer in me; they are safe for a while as this is close season.

Those bastard magpies have stripped the blackbirds nest clean! The nest in the dog rose, by the middle meadow. Of course, it could have been carrion crows but there are no shells near the nest. Crows would eat on the spot, mostly. Magpies are sneak-thieves and cowards. They burgle through the open back window, remove the booty and enjoy it far from the scene. Returning time and time again until there is no more. This was pied piracy, I am certain. *Pics pica* goes back to the top of the 'most wanted' list once again.

The yew trees on this estate are mighty and ancient. Especially those in the garden wood beneath the hall. I wish I could interview them; interrogate them on what they must have witnessed over the decades. Perhaps centuries? The stolen kisses and secret liaisons. The wander of beast and the roost of bird. The poachers and the gamekeepers. The ghosts and the will o' the wisps. I often feel watched in the garden wood ... and not just by the owls.

Purely by chance, I'm nearby as the suckling cows and their calves are released into the valley pasture; for the first time since birthing. The cattle have been confined to the mud and straw of the nursery compound for weeks. As the mothers trudge stoically down into the valley the calves gambol and frolic in the long, lush grass like spring lambs. Their reaction to freedom is a delight to witness. Then, after a while, a reality check. Two dozen calves start searching for their mothers. The bond between cow and calf is immense. It doesn't take long for each to pair off and order is restored.

They appear above the middle meadow during late morning. The hovering sun has triggered the hatch of a myriad invertebrates. The two birds dive-bomb the midges and mosquitoes relentlessly. Their aeronautic display is flawless, as always. My first swallows this year. I hope that the mud in the cattle nursery is still wet. They will need it for their nests in the farm buildings.

Passing under the old yew in the garden wood, there are three pairs of round eyes watching me. The tawny owl chicks have branched, ready to start their flying lessons. I move along quickly in case I panic them. They will fly when they are ready to. *"In nature, nothing hurries, yet everything is accomplished"*. Lao Tzu.

Staring at the sunset on the cusp between spring and summer, my find is full of expectation and excitement. I am at a 'cusp' in my own life, with much to consider. A long, successful and often stressful career in management has left its scars and I've chosen to 'retire'. Some call it 'leaving the rat race'. The challenge now is my financial obligations. Obligation, said a very wise man, is a form of slavery. No-one should live their lives as a slave. Should I 'cut my cloth' or find less demanding employment to fill the gap? Decisions, decisions.

The juicy green buds of elder and beech make lush fodder for the woodpigeons. They flutter and fuss, trying to balance long enough on slender boughs to wrestle free the shoots. Nature can be a wonderful benefactor in the simplest of ways. Just as the pigeons find easy pickings, so does the hunter. Who would deny me a tender, plump bird or two for my own table?

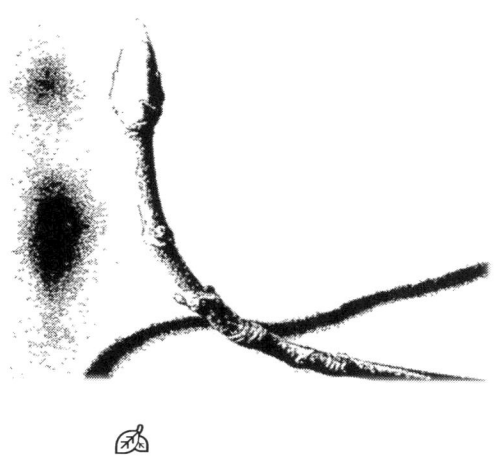

An early morning sortie around the outer fields and I'm searching for pheasants nests. Dylan, my lurcher, is meant to be assisting but is far more interested in nibbling at hare currants. A vegetarian delicacy for this canine. Knowing where the nests are helps me to protect them where I can. I'm following a beetle bank between two sprouting barley crops. An almighty 'boom' on the other side of the bank threatens to stop my heart. The lurcher, having jumped a foot and a half off the floor, is now half way across the county. I cover my ears while moving away and predictably (after thirty seconds) the second report sounds. I whistle loudly, recalling the dog, then waggle my fingers in my ears trying to relieve the compression. The woodpigeons, just two hundred yards away, continue tugging at the barley shoots. The bird scarer has had no effect at all.

The slender snow-white statue in the Garden wood pond isn't a swan. Its a little egret, with a little regret. Its mate hasn't arrived yet; but will be here soon. Smaller than a harnser with a narrow black bill and bright yellow slippers. Once only a migrant, it has become common in the East now and some pairs breed here. The bird was snatching tadpoles from the shallow water, her black eyes able to compensate for the refraction in the water and judge each strike perfectly.

A stump in a grassy clearing in the garden wood holds evidence of a master thief at work. Five plundered pheasant egg shells lie abandoned. I can only think of one nest-robber that might collect eggs and bring them to one place to feed. The crow is big and bold enough to eat on the spot. The stoat is incapable of carrying an egg. This is the work of a magpie, I'm sure.

May

May is the nesting month; the testing month. There are hundreds of tiny eggs in secret places now. Chaffinch, wren, blackcap, warbler, titmouse, robin, skylark and yellow-hammer. Every minor event, such as the carriage of food to the sitting hen or feeding chick, is watched by predators. They mark the live nest. Cowardly or clever? That isn't ours to call. It's Natures way. We can intervene or we can sit back and watch the drama. I refuse, though, to watch a whole hedgerow being pillaged of fledglings. So please forgive my occasional intervention.

The path past the pond in the garden wood is grassy and I slip through as quietly as a stalking panther. The grey ghost in the reed bed sees me, though. He croaks loudly, stopping my heart for a beat, then spreads his vast wings and lifts away. Old Frank is surprisingly agile and beats away behind the willows within seconds.

Wiping my bleary eyes I check the lawns again. My eyes don't deceive. The grass is alive with movement. I am watching the May-bug hatch. Dozens of tan-brown cockchafers, *Melolontha melolontha,* emerge from their subterranean nymph-skins to fly clumsily from the turf. The rooks have already seen them. So have the magpies. The bugs are poor aviators, buzzing noisily and blundering into each other. I withdraw to a distant hedge and watch the crows descend onto the greensward, shouting to their kin to join the feast. That mysterious bump on the bedroom window on a summer's eve? That will be a cockchafer bumbling blindly into the pane; Mother Natures Mr Magoo.

The blackbird nest in the dog-rose has resisted plunder. When I check today there are three blind, pink chicks and an egg not yet hatched. No sign of the hen but all looked healthy and well. I'm not the only one who can hear the plaintive begging of the chicks. A shifty black denizen is ghosting around in the high foliage above. A jackdaw. The Ethan Hunt of the avian world ... and this Mission isn't Impossible. It has seen me, yet its greed keeps it near. It can see the open yellow gapes of vulnerability. I accept the mission myself, retiring into cover to wait an eternity. Eventually Ethan can't resist an attempt at the chicks. A fatal mistake.

The distinctive call of the chiffchaff echoes around the beech grove on a delightfully sunny May morning. The drab little warbler escapes my view; it is often hard to pinpoint as it seems to 'throw' its voice. Is there any bird so synonymous with spring in the absence of the cuckoo?

Passing a newly cut conifer stump I stop to admire a very unusual insect. It's not the first time I've seen one, the last time having prompted me to learn more about it. It resembles a dark stick-insect in its strange posture ... head down, rear up in the air. It stands about two inches high. It is an Ichnuemon; a type of wasp. In particular, the species *Rhyssa persuasoria*. What the wasp is doing in this posture is one of Nature's minor wonders. It is using its ovipositor (no thicker than a human hair) to drill through the pine wood and reach the pupae of a horntail wasp which it has detected beneath the surface. The horntail egg was deposited in a borehole made and back filled by the wasp. The Ichnuemon egg will hatch on the horntail grub and its larva will feed on the host. To me, this is simply amazing. How can a simple wasp detect a pupae hidden within a wooden stump? How can such a fragile ovipositor drill through wood to place an egg with such accuracy?

I have a confession to make. I am a serial killer. My victims are pine-cones. There is no better elevated target for the practising rifle shooter. The activity is also eco-friendly; the dispersion of seed to the forest floor which encourages growth. Eden has a huge variety of conifer species, some with cones the size of a mans hand.

A pair of jackdaws have taken advantage of the arboriculture that keeps the estate safe and tidy. An exposed hollow in a trimmed bough makes for an ideal nesting spot for the jakes. A little obvious and exposed (to my hunters mind) but I will leave the pair alone. This is a nest for the photographer in me.

The inquisitive bird on the post between the coverts and the twelve-acre wood is a grey wagtail. I'm puzzled by its presence, which must be transient. This a bird normally seen at the side of the babbling brook or waterfall. There are neither here?

Although *'Phasianus colchicus'* is a physically awkward and often downright stupid bird, the pheasant is a master of disguise during the breeding season. Particularly the hens. Locating nests is no mean feat and often more easily done with a hound trained to the task. I wish I had such a dog at this time of the season. It makes nest protection so much easier. My old lurcher has always resisted tracking and retrieving 'feather'. Yet, today, he delights me by scenting out a nest containing eight olive eggs. They are laid in a hedgerow, on top of a segment of black plastic sack. I touch them, testing for warmth. They are stone cold. I break one and it's addled. The hen, I suspect, was a fox victim ... though Charlie obviously never found the nest.

The Meadow Witch again, loping along the edge of the growing barley. She will have leverets nearby, in a shallow scrape of earth. She appears a neglectful mother, her offspring lying exposed on open ground for the fox and the buzzard to find. She will only visit them once a day to let them suckle. Mortality is high in leverets but that is why she will bear two or three more broods this year. Survival through numbers.

The tawny owl chicks have dispersed. The boughs of the nesting tree, an old yew, are bare. I will miss their curious stare. The parent birds will remain in the area and I will see them now and again. Who knows where their progeny will establish territory? I wish them well.

The tawny owl and its favourite roost, the yew tree, combine harmoniously to conceal the bird until I'm right underneath her. Feather and bark blend perfectly. Only the languid blink of her liquid eyes gives away her presence.

I would guess that most wrens die of stress rather than predation. They are a strangely neurotic little bird; fretting at every movement within the wood. Don't get me wrong, I love wrens. Particularly their domed nest, a masterpiece of avian architecture. I watch one now, *'chitting'* around me. Chill out, Jenny! I'm here to protect you.

I cross the barbed wire fence above the cattle pasture. I retrieve my game-bag and rifle then set off, down into the long, verdant grass. Reaching the bottom of the low valley I glance right and spot three cattle lying about two hundred yards off. A cow, a calf and a bull ... which immediately lumbers to its feet. I'm in the centre of the meadow. My bag is laden with camera gear and the Weihrauch rifle is heavy. I suddenly have that 'too far from safety' feeling. The bull starts to snort as I pick up my pace, protesting my threat to his family. The shortest route to the wire is slightly uphill. A glance over my shoulder confirms that the beast is moving. I break into a trot. So does the bull. I break into a sprint. So does the bull. At the barbed wire I drop my bag over the top and slide the unloaded rifle onto it. I can hear the thunder of hooves and I stretch the top and middle barbed strands to allow me to roll through and land in a heap on the other side; two seconds later, 2000 lbs of prime beef slides to halt where I had just stood. I can feel the hot breeze from the beast's angry snorts. I stand up, trying to regain my dignity, and look at the heaving bull. His eyes tell me that he wasn't feinting. He paws angrily at the turf. I do a quick *'pasadoble'* shuffle, mutter "Ole'!" and head for the wood.

The buzzards often follow me around, particularly when they have young in the nest. The oldest male has long come to learn that rather than threat, I am a source of sustenance. I happily supply shot squirrels at strategic, easily seen locations. This, I hope , deflects raptor attention away from the pheasant poults. Today the ancient hawk *mewls* above the forest, knowing I am somewhere below and we speak to each other. I mimic his query using my Foxcaller. The squirrels are confused. Buzzards above and buzzards below. Occasionally *Buteo buteo* sweeps into the wood to check my progress. He needn't worry. There will be meat on top of the midden pile, as always.

I haven't heard a single cuckoo yet; though May is still young. Is the decline of the cuckoo a good thing or bad? In that it reflects the equal decline of the meadow pipit, it must be bad. The loss of the song, that two-tone clarion call to Summer; that is what seems truly sad.

Occasionally, the estate is surveyed by some birders (probably the BTO ... British Trust for Ornithology) with the owner's permission. If I'm warned, I make myself scarce. Birders just don't understand gun-controlled, target specific conservation efforts. I would like to think their report reads *"Evidence of lots of songbirds but very few corvids?"* (Blows on finger-nails and polishes them on lapel).

Out along one of the dykes in the water meadow, the mute swans have nested. The cob is browsing on the turf while the pen sits watching me careful. The nest is huge, damming the shallow waterway.

Along the North Drive, a column of ornamental trees guard the route. Today they are in full blossom under a glorious sun. Pink, white, yellow ... the uniforms worn with dignity and pride. A host of solitary bees, hover flies, honey bees and bumble bees are nectar gathering amongst the florets. The buzz and hum is entrancing. A symphony to early summer. A grand day to be alive.

A carrion crow has found a pheasant's scant nest between some coppiced stumps. I watch from a distance, not through lenience but wanting to find the answer to a question often asked of me. Does the crow eat at the scene of the crime (risking conflict with an adult pheasant) or does it steal away with each egg? The answer, I witness today, is both. *Corvus corone* is a big, powerful bird. It will plunder in-situ until disturbed, when it will stab a shell and lift it away to gorge in anonymity.

She holds her calm and her position until the last second. Only as I brush past the thorny briars does she panic and explode from the tangle. Her alarm call, as she brushes my ear, makes my heart leap in my chest; such is the proximity and surprise. I gently part the briars and there it is. The blackbirds nest; complete with a clutch of four speckled eggs. I look about furtively. Not like a sneak-thief but like a sentinel. I pray that the magpies aren't watching from afar.

I'm watching the Meadow Witch browsing out on the lea close to the pine wood. Tonight will be the May full moon. The Hare Moon. Will my little witch be gazing at the silver orb in awe? There is much folklore around the moon-gazing hare, from fertility to alchemy. All I know is this. While there is a full May moon ... and a hare to watch it ... all is well in the world.

May is the month of the wild hyacinth. '*Hyacinthoides non-scripta*' seems a dismal classification for such an iconic plant. I stand in the garden wood drowning in an ocean of bluebells. Already roe, squirrel and badger have violated this display with their trampling and foraging. Grey squirrels and badgers love to dig up the succulent bulbs. Thankfully there are thousands more bluebell tubers than hungry badgers. Nature takes care of such conflicts. I have a testing question for the reader, though. Why do we call them 'bluebells'? To my eye, as I stand here surveying a wondrous scene, the flowers seem lilac. I suspect that the poets and scriveners of yore preferred 'bluebell' to 'lilac-bell'. It just rolls off the tongue better. Or perhaps I'm colour blind?

Those much recorded 'darling buds of May' push forth on shrub and tree. The eruption of lush, green growth excites the heart. The chasing away of winters dreary grip. In the forest, amongst the leaf mulch at floor level, the tendrils of a million 'triffids' burst through. They uncurl as they stretch upwards at a rate of two or three inches a day. The 'tick-trees' ... the brackens and ferns that will soon drown the untrodden ground.

The old lurcher refused to be drawn away from the hedgerow. His nose was buried beneath a blackthorn, exploring a dry ditch. I stepped up expecting to find a pheasant's nest but instead found an abandoned crown. A roebuck skull, cleaned of flesh and bleached by Nature. I gave the old dog a pat on the head. He knew, though, that there would be negotiation ahead before the lovely mistress of the house would allow this on the study shelf. As I write, it is still in the garden shed ...

A small sad bundle of black fur lies on the badger trail, yet ignored by Brocks nocturnal scouring. The dead mole, the little gentleman in the velvet coat, has seemingly died of natural causes. I find these occasionally. I have a theory, though not proven. The heart attack, I suspect, is caused by chance contact with a high predator. Like shrews, moles seem to have something in their make-up that leaves them obnoxious to predators. If a fox or badger were to 'toy' with a mole caught above surface the creature would be terrified.

A swift encounter down along the feeder brook. The dog fox stares through the grass at me before leaping the brook and running out across the water meadow.

June

The rabbit's vision is imperfect due to the design of its skull. Approach it head-on and (like its big cousin, the hare) it might not even see you. Especially if preoccupied with feeding like the big-eyed doe I walked up to today. It was her nose that warned her I was near and she stood up on her haunches to sniff the air. Luckily for her my interest was only in capturing her image on this fair summer morning.

Picking a path between the barley and the briar's, I wend my way down towards the river gate. I stop for a while to study a small, sylvan cone woven between the thorny stems. It is cleverly placed close to a blossom of white bramble flowers. Inside the conical web I can see the cluster of innumerate eyes above a set of fierce mandibles. The monster watching me is a funnel-web spider. It is waiting to spring on a juicy and unsuspecting hover-fly, seeking out nectar.

In the searing sun I can hear the crack and spit of the warming conifers above my head. Before long I'm rubbing my eyes. The pine pollen is shedding. Then I chance upon a blackcaps nest, when the hen deserts it as I pass a low briar patch. Pulling back the thorns and leaves gently, I count five tiny mottled eggs.

A fox emerges from the twelve-acre wood; no semblance of vigilance or stealth. I squat quickly and lay the lurcher beside me. Charlie picks his way across the beet field, pausing now and then to snatch a grub or beetle. Indignantly, he stops to squat and scat on top of a sugar beet plant (one sugar or two, madam?). The lurcher beside me is bristling, his hunting genes can't be neutralised by unnatural law, only training and restraint. The fox is moving steadily towards the pheasant coverts where many newly fledged poults are following hens. Though the fox isn't my legitimate quarry, I can still intervene. I stand and whistle loudly, spreading my arms. Old Charlie halts and turns towards the sound, looking disdainful. I lift the rifle and plug a pellet into a tree branch just twenty feet in front of his intended path into the covert. The fox leaps in surprise and runs back from whence he came. I step from the tree-line with the dog and out into the beet crop. Charlie gets the firm message and canters off. A rudely healthy dog fox, deterred for a short time, at least.

The June sun has parched the puddle-mud and trapped, until the next deluge, the forensic evidence of passing fauna. *Meles meles* can never deny that he paused at the pool. His gait was steady, back paw placed almost on top of the print of the fore paw. A relaxed, meandering gait. He was probably hoovering up the ugly black slugs that lie like goblin turds along the rides. The badger's diet is hugely omnivorous. In fact, almost unlimited. A peeled hedgehog, an excavated rabbit kit, a fat slug, a prised open sweet chestnut, the low lying blackberry or the windfall apple. All in a nights work for Britain's little 'bear'.

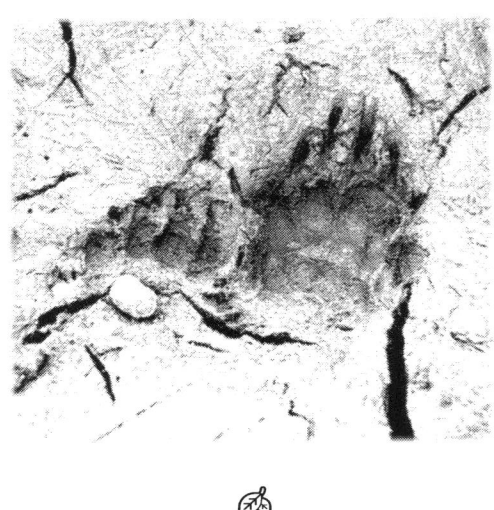

Along the edges of the flint-walled descent to the garden wood, a leggy plant stands aloft with a pretty mid-blue flower. The striking colour contradicts the blandness of nettle and flint. It is chicory, the blue daisy. Its roots were once roasted and blended with coffee to make a bitterer brew. Cast a chicory flower onto an ant's nest and the attack of the insects will turn it pink. Their formic acid brings out the litmus property of the petals.

The tiny bird sitting on a fence rail near the water meadows shouldn't be there! I'm only used to seeing it in the vertical position ... not the horizontal. It doesn't appear happy with my appearance and fusses about. I have stepped too close to the tree-creepers nest, I suspect.

If every tree that died just toppled and lay there waiting for ice and wind and rain to erode it, we wouldn't be able to move for dead boles. Mother Nature is far too clever to allow that. Instead she gives us a break-down and clean-up squad. The turkey-tail and root-rot fungi are part of that team; slowly eating away at the lifeless timber and returning nutrients to the soil.

I watch a hare on the cattle pasture. This is a new character to me. He has his nose down following the pheromones of the Meadow Witch. He is a huge young buck, the size of a Norfolk terrier. The Witch will appreciate his contribution to her gene-pool, for he is a handsome specimen. He senses me and watches me through the bars of the gate for a minute or two, his ears searching for sound and nostrils scenting. At the snap of the camera shutter the hare explodes into flight; Usain Bolt on the starters gun. I would put his odds of chasing down the Meadow Witch at 6/4 on. She will enjoy his virility.

Sometimes I dwell on Eden long enough to complete my figure-of-eight patrol. This is the 'Full Monty'. The 'big breakfast'. The indulgence. It allows me to check the margins, the coverts, the rides and the hollows. From the woodshed, through the farmyard, into the plantation and out to the pine wood. Down through the pine wood to the brook, then along it. Across the cattle pasture into the garden wood and back up to the woodshed. Then out along the paths to the Firecrest covert, out through twelve-acre wood. East along the estates perimeter, towards the river. Back along the bottom of the escarpment and up through the trees to the wood shed. A healthy three mile plus circuit, packed with the opportunity to observe wildlife. This is why I love Eden so much.

A whitethroat chastises me from a low elder branch as I pass too close to its nest. A sadly revealing trait in smaller songbirds, which often results in the nest being found by the predators they seek to divert. In this case, the bird is lucky. I will try to keep an eye out for the magpie and the crow.

A carrion crow is stalking through the beech plantation. Guessing it will be up to mischief I watch it for a while. It is hunting for woodpigeon nests, I'm sure. In my biased eyes, a fairly useful occupation for a crow!

There is a prowler in the long grass, near the old orchard. I'm watching from away up the escarpment, my scent high above its range. I know there are pheasant poults in there. So does the fox. You don't shoot Old Charlie with airguns but you can interfere positively in their mischief. The smack of a .22 pellet in a fence post close to the foxes position sends the poults scurrying away and makes Charlie flee.

The foxgloves are in flower; *Digitalis purpurea*. These proud plants stand like royalty in the beech grove, reaching the height of a man. They are a favourite with hover-flies and solitary bees. Yet there is, as we know, a dark side to the foxglove. A source of poison and a killer of kings and queens.

I'm in cover down near the feeder brook when a harnser lands nearby. She has seen my pigeon decoys and watches them from a safe distance. What a wonderful old girl! Her presence gives some passing woodies the confidence to sweep down and land among the decoys. Sadly, once the first pigeon rolls over in a puff of feathers, the heron opens her vast wings and sweeps away with a croak of protest.

Sitting in cover watching pigeons out on the rain-flattened barley, the relentless industry of a pair of long-tailed tits draws my interest. They are bringing food to the young in a nest, their tiny beaks crammed with midges and fruit-flies. The nest ... a luxurious ball of moss and cattle hair ... is woven ingeniously into the reeds standing along the brook. Feeling intrusive, I vacate and change my shooting position. There is a fragility here that demands respect. I would rather go home with an empty bag than disturb this dainty family.

Walking beside the drainage brook, a trill melody emanates from the willows. Stopping to listen I'm reminded of a time some fifty years ago (when such things were loosely tolerated). A ten year old egg-collector had watched the reed warblers through a pair of cheap plastic Woolworth's binoculars. I never did locate that first warbler nest but hours of watching taught me their song. The juvenile nest searching was my baptism into hunting and I learned much about birds. Across the years, time well spent in the hunting field has taught me a great deal about both birds and mammals. Now I know far more than I should ... but still less than I want to. The warbler obliged me with a photograph today. Far more rewarding than an empty eggshell.

It is late morning in twelve-acre wood and shafts of sunlight break between the conifer boles. A million insects are suddenly highlighted, hovering like dust-motes above the bracken leaves. The forest is warm with light and alive activity. It hums to the symphony of Natures orchestra.

Squatting beneath the blackthorns to target pigeons out on the field, I hear the crack of a twig behind me and come alert. I turn slowly and see a form moving through the nettle beds. I prop the gun against a tree trunk and slip the camera from the game-bag. The muntjac buck comes within four yards of my natural hide and only the subtle snap of the cameras shutter turns it away to flee.

The bundle of fur on the gate post is an owl pellet. Barn owl, I suspect. Like a schoolboy, I pocket the treasure. At home, I carefully dismantle it to examine the contents. I find that the owl had a good night, with two voles on the menu.

A rarely seen bird caught my attention today. Song thrushes used to be ten-a-penny in my youth; as common as blackbirds. Their decline is as sad as that of the corncrake and the hedgehog. I used to regularly find the thrushes 'anvil'. The stone or stump where the bird would hold snails in its bill and smash open the shells. Why the heavy decline when snails are plentiful? Could it be due to the prevalence of lungworms in molluscs? I don't have the answer but to hear and see the thrush today was a delight.

Hidden somewhere in the garden wood is my *'tree of life'*. I pass it often and when the sun is bright it emanates a rubicund glow from its paper-thin flaky bark. It is a Chinese maple tree; *Acer hersii*. The tree oozes the spirit of the Tao. I always touch it when I pass.

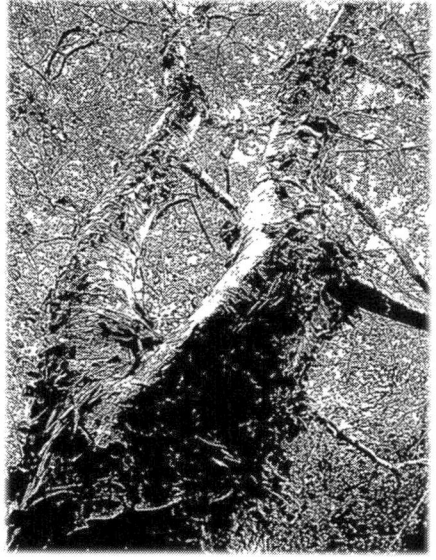

Seeking shade from a searing sun, I find a cool spot in the Garden Wood. The lurchers lungs are heaving under his thick coat (an inheritance from his Bedlington grandmother). The arboretum is thick with yew, pine, beech and shrubs such as rhododendron and azalea. This is the coolest part of the whole estate and at river level too. As I offer the dog water from my bottle, we disturb the Wood Witch from her damp cover in a bed of ramsons. She sits up to stare at me. I carefully lift the camera from my bag and use the telephoto lens to look deep into her eye. It is liquid brown, a pool of mystique and wild wisdom. Her eye seems to be trying to probe my mind, interrogate my intent. I slowly lower the camera, adjust the lens and raise it to take a picture. She poses for me perfectly; Greta Garbo. Then she lopes off gently, silently, into the depths of the dark wood.

The unmistakable rise and cadent descent of the male chaffinch's song rings out like a plea for response across the previously silent copse. *Fringilla coelebs* was once trapped in Victorian times to sing in cages. Rival cocks were wagered on in gloomy taverns, the winner being the one that sang the most verses within a judged timescale. The sort of taverns that promoted dog-fights, rat-pits and cock-fighting.

Old Charlie has been up to more mischief, for sure. What rural crime is he fleeing now? What sin has been committed? He has nothing in his jaws ... so perhaps he was interrupted before murder most foul. Or should that be murder most fowl?

The early morning scout along the escarpment pays an unexpected dividend. A barn owl is quartering the middle meadow in the half-light. A moon-faced spectre floating a few feet above the half-grown hay. A soundless, unhurried bird in flight. The ninja of the meadows. She circles once more. At the cusp between hay and farrow, she swoops upwards slightly. Then plunges, talons outstretched, wings tucked back behind her. I hold my breath as she remains out of sight. Then she rises, a vole clamped in one talon. The catch is carried up and over the old orchard, towards the Old Hall. There will be young to feed there. The nest in one of the out-buildings, I'm certain.

The chatter of a passing magpie leaves curious. What crime has been committed? Who was the victim? For when the magpie is abroad, there will always be a victim.

The brimstone blossom on the twig at the top of the gorse bush is singing its heart out. "Chiz-iz-iziz-iziz-iziz-eeez". A cock yellow bunting, Emberiza citrinella, marking his territory and looking for love. One of the most striking British birds. We all know it as the yellowhammer but in some areas it is called the 'scribble lark' due to the pencil-like markings on its eggs.

The sensation of something watching me isn't new, by any means. As I stalk the coverts and thickets, it's *'see or be seen'*. Standing at the foot of a sturdy yew tree, I glance up into its branches. There are not one, but three, pairs of wide eyes staring back at me. A trio of tawny owlets have left the nest and branched. Three balls of downy plumage, awaiting food and far, far yet from independence. I slide away silently, lest I panic them into premature flight. A magical encounter.

A common and attractive plant found throughout Eden during summer is the rosebay willowherb. Few realise that wasn't originally a wild, hedgerow plant. It originated as a garden plant in Victorian times but its light seeds spread easily and it's now widely seen.

A fragile looking bird objects to my intrusion as I cross the farmyard. Twitching its tail as it nags me, it runs in front with little sprints then stops to chitter again. A handsome little complainer; best admired and never ignored. The pied wagtail won the day as I let him chase me off, as always. It's good for his ego.

Heron, harnser, Old Frank ... any of the three names are widely used in Norfolk. I watch this one as it stilt-walks along the water meadows edge. It stops, statuesque, from time to time. Then another pause and the long neck strikes like an arrow into a nettle bed. A hen pheasant breaks cover, her alarm call ringing around the river valley. In its spear-like bill, the harnser holds a poult. Then I see something I've never seen before ... or since. The hen pheasant attacks the huge heron, flying at its legs with the ferocity of a fighting cock. Two, three times it slashes at the kidnapper who lifts off, carrying the struggling poult. As it gains speed the brave hen follows, trying to land on the grey bandits back. Alas, the predator out-flies the courageous mother bird. The pheasant returns to her brood. She hasn't saved the chick but I suspect she has just saved the rest of her offspring.

There is something out-of-place in the ripe sugar beet crop. I stop to study it and realise that there are actually four things. All tawny, in marked contrast to the verdant beet leaves. Ears! A handsome roe kid stands up. Then a second one rises and they return my stare. Four wide eyes, two twitching noses. Twins ... proverbial peas from the same pod. A bark resounds from the margin of a nearby spinney and out steps their mother. I make myself scarce.

There is a bristle and buzz about the field margins. Solitary bees, bumble bees, honey bees and hover flies are everywhere on this warm summer afternoon. The thistle heads are in flower and the insects are gathering nectar.

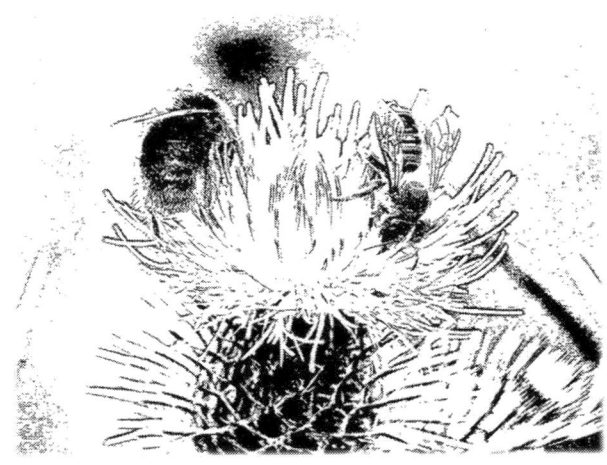

The hairy stemmed plant looks strangely out of place at the woods margin. A lonely specimen which has seemingly lost its tribe. Common comfrey is a flower of the water-meadow and riverbank, where its species flourish. Herbalists of old used to pulverise its roots to make plaster to set broken bones. Hence the nickname 'knitbone' used by some country folk.

My seat for the insect ballet is 'up in the gods'. Only because I can't get closer to the pool, hindered by nettle and weed. The pond skaters, *Gerris lacustris,* are dancing for their dinner, scavenging for drowned insects on the ponds surface. Water striders, they step briskly across the surface tension caused by the polarity of the waters molecules. The microscopic hairs on their legs trap air bubbles which, if the water surface gives way, act as a natural buoyancy aid.

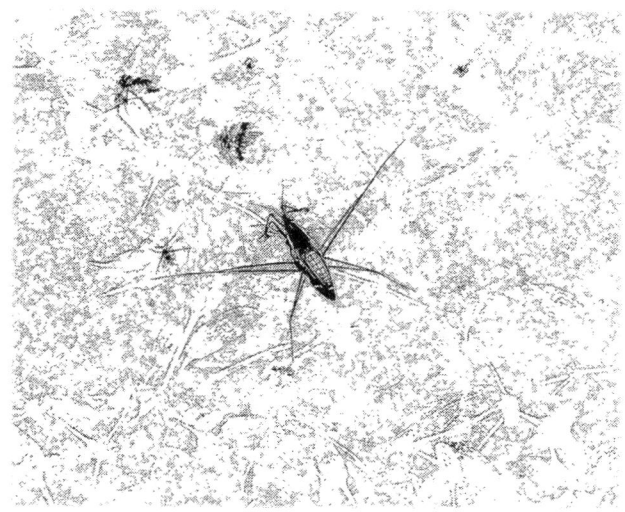

Deep in the nettle beds, a beautiful and delicate creature roosts at night throughout the summer. Sit and watch the nettles by the South-facing wall of the old orchard during mid-morning and they will emerge to feed and sunbathe. By mid-day they will have attained enough nutrition for the afternoon dance. The courtship dance. The males will engage in gentle combat to secure territories. The afternoon will be spent pursuing the flirty females and mating. From late afternoon to dusk they will all feed again before retiring into the nettles to sleep. Not a bad life really, for *Nymphalis urticae* ... the Small Tortoiseshell butterfly. Sleep, eat, sex, eat, sleep!

If there is anyone that knows Eden more intimately than me now, it is old Ralph, the gardener. They told me today he's had a stroke and isn't faring too well. I feel deeply for him. Such an event, at his ripe age, is unlikely to see the old boy return to duty. Yet, present or absent, his mind (like mine) will always wander here among the trees and rides. I will miss the sound of Ralph's vintage tractor trundling up the track to seek me out. We enjoyed a yarn. Ralph, too, knows where the badgers dig and the buzzards nest. Where the vixen dug her nursery den and where the tawny owl sits on eggs. The trunk which holds the woodpecker's chicks and where the roe fawn lies in cover. Keep well, old chap ... and please come back when you can.

A wide tractor trail runs between two crop fields from the farm to twelve-acre wood. The ground is arid and dusty. I come across half a dozen tall, striking plants. A species common to Norfolk heaths … but the first I've seen on this estate. They are in flower already, the stout stems draped in a cascade of deep purplish blue. Each flower has a long scarlet stamen. It is Vipers-bugloss, *Echium vulgae.* The plants seeds resemble an adders head and were believed by the ancients to be an antidote to snake venom. Hence the plants unusual name. One of my favourite wild flowers.

Lying prone in the grass on a hot afternoon, I'm watching rabbits through my riflescope. A green blur fills my vision and I raise my head, confused. In front of me, a meadow grasshopper has climbed up a stalk to look down the scope. Its comical stare makes me grin.

Striding the sandy track between a maize cover crop and the wood I see what looks like a black stone. The stone scuttles away, feeling the vibration of my approach. It starts digging into the sand, seeking refuge below ground. It is a Minotaur beetle, *Typhaeus typhoeus* ... a type of antlered dung beetle and one of our largest.

July

As always on the return from the summer wood, I check the dog for ticks. His thick coat both attracts and easily hides these loathsome little organisms. The deer tick. *Ixodes ricinus*. They are prolific in the woods I walk not just because of their affinity with deer but also with the badgers. The tick will host on and drink the blood of any mammal. When gorged, their abdomen fills with blood and they puff up like a tiny grey balloon. Thus they are often called the 'castor bean'. I find four on the dog; one already anchored and gorging. A twist of my little green O' Tom tool separates the jaws from my dog's skin. The others are plucked off between finger and thumb. All are destroyed. I check my shirt, suspicious now. There are two crawling beneath my collar, searching for my neck. I crush them under-heel on a concrete slab. I have twice been tested for Lyme disease after illness following tick-bites. Thankfully both tests were negative. Beware the tiny tick. We are often just a bite away from invalidity or death. This is Lucifer's circus-flea, for sure.

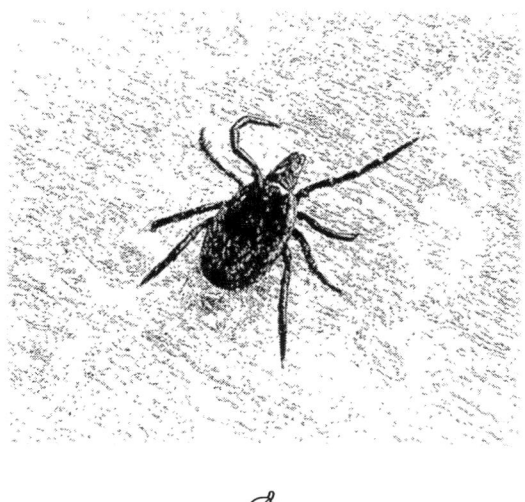

The heat shimmer along the clay-baked track makes focus difficult. I'm sure that in the space between the stands of growing maize I can see a squatting rabbit? Conies are few and far between on this estate, the previously fecund warrens gassed out years ago, I'm told. I study the form again then raise the rifle to look through the scope. It's a tussock with a couple of deer-stolen maize kernels leaning against it. I shoot the Aunt Sally coney. A magnificent shot! One of the cobs tumbles. Cruelly, I send the dog in to retrieve and the old boy canters to the 'kill'. He stands over it quizzically and sniffs at the bloodless vegetation. I call him back and pat his puzzled head. With my eyesight and his speed, every wild thing in Norfolk ought' be safe.

The warning comes early, from that most reliable forecaster, the stormcock. The mistle thrush perches on the highest sprig of the tallest cedar, puffing out its speckled waistcoat to herald the god of thunder. Layers of rolling grey cumuli stack above the landscape. An ethereal tsunami. Soon the distant rumbles amplify. The flash, the count, the race of pulse. Inside the wood, under a double umbrella of beech and yew leaves, watching the lightning forks is supernatural entertainment. Beneath bright strike and cannon crash every wild beast is silent; tremulous, sheltering. The rain slaps relentlessly at the verdant canopy. Then it passes, rumbling and growling, into the East. All that is left behind is sound and scent. The drip of the raindrop sliding from the waxy leaf and the sweet, luscious scent of sodden turf.

The snaking river and its margins supply the ideal habitat for a host of dragonflies and damselflies. The species list is impressive. Common darters, Norfolk hawkers, ruddy darters, Southern hawkers, emperor dragonflies, azure and common blue damselflies, banded demoiselles, emerald damselflies. Buzzing and hovering in the sunshine. Squadrons of little helicopters blitzing the midges like a scene from Apocalypse Now, but without the napalm. The Darters are so named because they lurk on the vegetation at launch at passing prey. The Hawkers do exactly that; constantly on the wing hunting down and chasing their prey. There is a fairly easy way to tell the difference between a dragonfly and a damselfly though it only works when they are still. Dragonflies can't fold their wings, so they remain stretched out at rest. Damselflies (and demoiselles are small damselflies) will tuck their wings back along the body while static. Also the demoiselles and damselflies are smaller and more slender than their dragonfly cousins. Often they will be coupled, looking like a flying wheel.

I'm sitting at the edge of the twelve-acre wood, in the shade. The sky is azure, cloud free, pure ... except for the buzzards. The pair are now three and they wheel together, high up on the thermals. When I came to Norfolk eighteen years ago, *buteo buteo* was as rare as hen's teeth across most of the county. Now, they have migrated here in numbers, from the West. They, like me, seem to have realised that Norfolk is one of the last bastions of the big sky. Their cries, high above, give a wild edge to the skyscape. I pull my Foxcaller from my pocket and mimic their mewling. Slowly, cautiously, they descend and introduce me to the new member of the family. Out of respect, I cast a brace of squirrel cadavers into the meadow and move away through the trees.

By mid-morning, the height of Old Sol is casting sunbeams down through the canopy; searchlights around a verdant battlefield. Perhaps the border guards of suburban mediocrity have realised I've gone missing? Maybe my employer is searching for my soul, knowing they don't own it and never, ever will. Thousand of flying beasties dance a ballet within the shafts of light. Tiny Valkyries with a defined choreography. They start low, at the base of the beam, and then spiral up towards the canopy. Then they free fall and start the dance again. The sequence of life. The pattern of Mother Nature. Rise and fall. Ebb and flow. Live and die.

Passing along the base of the escarpment, I stop to check the blackcap's nest I found last month. Expecting to find fledglings all I find is an empty nest. I search the ground beneath and around the nest. There are no feathers and no eggshells. Nothing. Was it a magpie or stoat? I will never know for sure but my head says magpie. They lift their plunder away to ransack it, whereas the stoat would break the eggs on the spot. The lack of eggshells also tells me the birds never even got to hatch.

A little piece of magic lights my day. Stopping and sitting on a log to take a draft of cold water, a miniscule bird appears. It's chasing midges and mites on the dropping cedar leaves. The golden stripe on its crown identifies the second smallest bird in Britain. The goldcrest; *Regulus regulus*. Then I'm blessed further as the rest of the family appears, fussing around the evergreens.

Two weeks without rain starts to take its toll on leaf and land. The almost constant breeze, like a Mediterranean mistral, whips up dust-devils along the tractor trails. The pipes will be out soon, I'm sure; the irrigation system, to save the potato crops. The puddles from the last summer rains have long since evaporated or been lapped up by bird and beast. Deer, rabbits and squirrels have been bark stripping … craving moisture. The leaves of the ash are turning alarmingly. Not through 'dieback' disease but through pure dehydration.

A pair of linnets entertain me, diving from a perch in a budding sapling into the thistle heads to feed then returning to the tree to sing; a celebration of their contentment. The linnet has a wonderful song, reminiscent of a trickling mountain brook. Like the chaffinch it was long abused for its vocal talent in Victorian times, confined to tiny cages in the parlours of the gentry. Thankfully such days are gone; the linnets and chaffinches are far more threatened by the sparrowhawk now than man.

How strange that in the sun-kissed summer wood, it is usually the weightless and most silent thing that the hunter carries with them that gives away their presence. Nor can they divest it, with ease. It also, sometimes, betrays the incoming bird to the waiting hunter. You can't touch it, smell it or hear it. Yet its presence is unavoidable. Everything, whether alive or inert has one, when there is light of any kind. It is, of course, a shadow.

A damp summer morning, humming with midges and a sudden chance encounter with a roe doe under the escarpment. She is a creature of deep beauty and I can immediately understand why people use the expression 'doe-eyed'. She studies me for a minute or two before sauntering off up the incline. Magic.

In the hedgerows and along the walled tracks, there are sprinklings of Red Campion; *Silene dioica*. The Latin name derives from a Greek god, Silenus. A drunken merrymaker of the woods.

All creatures need to hydrate. Water, which makes the greater mass of every mammal and bird, is essential to health and survival. How creatures come by their water can be varied, opportunistic, innovative or just plain simple. The squirrel will lap at the rainwater pool caught in the roots of the beech tree. The rabbit will sup the dew from the doc leaves. The magpie will splash and sip at the muddy pool in the tractor rut. The game-birds on Eden are lucky in having an ancient system of brick built feeders, designed into the landscape by some long lost genius. They are set at points where rainwater runs off from higher ground to replenish them naturally. They had been lost beneath undergrowth but have now been restored. Of course it won't just be the pheasants that drink at these. Every passing creature can benefit from the small, accessible wells.

It's nearly half a century since I last dropped rose-hip seeds down the back of a friend's shirt or, indeed, had them pushed down mine! A nasty schoolboy prank guaranteed to make your back itch for hours. I'm reminded now by the dainty pink petals and yellow stamens of the dog roses in the hedgerow. The Tudor rose and the main ingredient of rose-hip syrup. A shrub believed by the Ancient Greeks to cure rabies from a dog bite, hence the 'dog' misnomer.

There is a hive of industry in an oak tree ... literally. A honey bee colony has nested in a hole about five feet from the ground. The drones are entering and exiting in their dozens so I distance myself and watch. At least they've had the sense to choose a site for the hive where it is impenetrable to badgers.

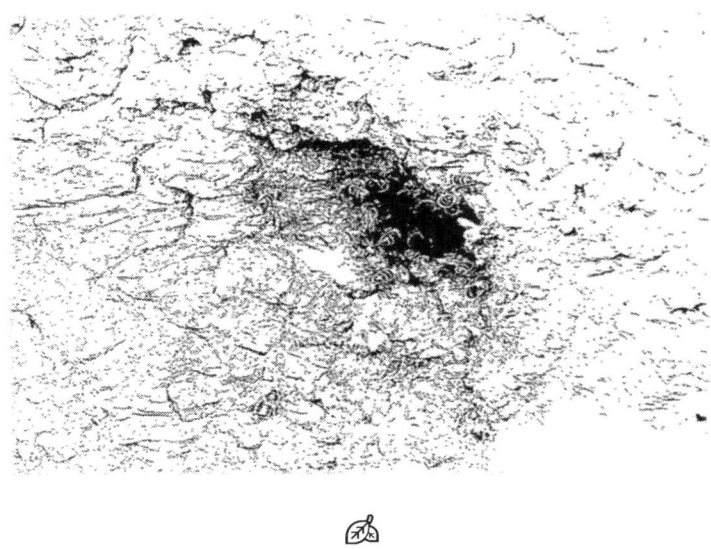

The small warren in the plantation is progressing slowly. It's certainly not me inhibiting its growth. It is disease and (perhaps) natural predation. I only say perhaps because there is little evidence of fox or badger predation in the vicinity. What have we done, we humans? Myxomatosis and VHD (Viral Haemorrhagic Disease) are vile consequences of our historic interventions on Nature.

A shallow brook bypasses the main river and feeds the garden wood pond. Only when the river is in flood does the brook fill enough to harbour a few tiddlers. Enough to occasionally draw a heron or egret to the pond. Today I'm blessed with a little arrow from the gods. A blaze of sapphire that streaks towards me and lands on a dead twig overhanging the brook. Luckily I have the camera, not the gun, in my hand.

I walk the sultry margins in a sweat, keeping half an eye on the swifts. The other half is on the rolling cloud bank over the horizon. The humidity is cloying. The swifts have descended, following the millions of airborne insects being pushed earthward by the weather front. I turn back fast, heading in the direction of the motor. The swifts are now hawking at ground level and the sky is dark with threat. Before I reach the car, a fork of lightning carves through the black skyscape; the summer storm has struck.

In the humid pine wood, man and dog progress with lolling tongues and the drip of perspiration. A host of Valkyries nip and bite at my salty skin; skin devoid of any chemical protection because I simply forgot the lotion. I halt the dog with a quiet flick of the fingers. I've noticed a dark, languid form beneath a tree. She is sunbathing; sleeping in a sunbeam ... topping up her tan. It is the Wood Witch. We creep past and leave her undisturbed.

What god-forsaken purpose is there to the midge? What have midges ever done for us, besides plague the air and bite the unclad skin? "Well ... they feed the wren and hawking swift or swallow." Yes, but " ... and they serve that rare and noble flying mouse, the bat." I know, but" ... and what would feed the Norfolk hawker and the ruddy darter dragonflies, if not for creatures like the humble midge? I concede and continue to rub witch-hazel gel into the affected area.

While staking out a squirrel drey in the garden wood, I notice a movement to my right. I'm tucked behind a yew, out of sight. My eye is drawn to a rotten pine stump, about twelve feet high. The top of the tree has long since toppled and rotted, no doubt a victim of ring-barking by the squirrels. Something has entered a hole drilled about two feet down from the top of the stump. Expecting to see a woodpecker emerge, I'm surprised when a jackdaws head appears at the exit with a pink, squeaking, featherless chick in its bill. It flies off. I hurry to the stump and put my ear to it. There are more hungry, pleading chicks in there. I resume my position, deciding to let nature take its course and learn from what I see. Five minutes later the jackdaw returns and takes another chick. Within twenty minutes, the jake has cleared the woodpeckers nest. Nature in the raw, no quarter given and red in tooth and claw.

A large black pirate sails along the line of the river, its long neck outstretched as its wings cut the air. The cormorant has come far inland to plunder the nearby trout fisheries. Anglers, of course, resent the birds presence and I have much sympathy for them. Cormorants are amazingly efficient fish hunters.

I spot the young fox, little more than a yearling, hunting voles in the long grass. It is missing every time but looks in rude health. I duck into cover, ready my camera and use my 'mouse squeaker' to attract the cub's attention. It sprints in towards the hedgerow where I'm hiding and stops, looking quizzically, trying to figure out what is making the noise?

A stalk along the flinty margin betwixt the half-grown maize and the blackthorn hedge. A hint of tawny fur between the canes brings me to a halt. There is a devil in the deep green sea; cloven hoof and horned head. The beast has seen me and deliberates in its flight. The harsh hedgerow or the open crop? It makes its decision. Three leaps and it is through the blackthorn, away up the escarpment. *Muntiacus reevesi*; the muntjac deer.

A comma drifts by and settles on a briar blossom. It diverts my attention from the ambush in which I'm engaged. The 'what is' is more important than the 'what might be'. I stop to count the variety of butterflies along the hedgerow. Brimstone, tortoiseshell and small white. A red admiral, as befits Nelsons county. Essex skipper, gatekeeper and peacock. My favourite is the comma, but why? Because I am a writer and the comma is such an important tool. The comma emphasises the text to follow, with its momentary pause. Today, my comma emphasised the need to pause and take in the beauty surrounding me.

Poised at the end of the drive just before sunset, I sit and marvel at the view. The sea of ripening barley is bathed in a blood-red hue as the sun descends in the West. Above the crop, pipistrelle and Daubenton bats are busy harvesting the evening insect hatch. A feast ... and a fanfare to the fading day. Yet another bountiful day it has been, too.

It's unusually cold for a July morning and I blow on my chilled fingers. Striking out from the plantation, I pass a pile of reeking, steaming cattle bedding. Straw, squit and piss combining to blend an aroma dominated by ammonia. *Eau de bovine*. The heap has been growing over the weeks as the empty cattle shed has been cleaned out. I've knocked a few crows off the top recently as they foraged for dung beetles. To my utter surprise, a roe kid is lying comfortably on top, watching the dog and I pass. Not a new born; a juvenile. The curtain of stink had obviously cloaked our scent. The young deer was clearly enjoying the heat from the warm mound and seemed reluctant to leave. I pulled the old lurcher away (he still hadn't seen the deer) and left the resourceful beast to its leisure.

August

A spray of ochre dust billows atop the hedgerows as I drive along the winding lanes. What looks like a golden sandstorm is my invitation to several weekends sport. The barley harvest has begun and those huge monsters of industry, the combines, are cutting day and night. No more the hay-wain, horse and hand-held scythe. These machines can cut and grade with finite skill, steered by satellites looking down upon the Earth from lord knows where? Yet even this level of precision leaves surplus spoil. The pigeon and the crow will venture down when the leviathans depart.

Rolled bales, square bales, single bales, heaped bales. Haystacks or silage rows. I love them all. Hide-outs and pigeon butts. Straw and warmth. Shelter and secrecy. I've always loved the straw stacks. I can remember my mother shaking loose straw from my teenage jeans and asking what on earth I'd been up to? I suspect my girlfriends mother asked the same of her. Halcyon days. Warm autumn skies and first fumbling's. The sight of the harvest and the scent of the bales infuse the same lust for life that I had back then.

A skulking rat beneath the hedgerow can have no legitimate business I can think of. Mischief is afoot so I hold a one-man kangaroo court, find the rat guilty of suspicious behaviour and condemn it to death. Unusually for me, I miss! *Rattus norvegicus* lives to plunder more eggs; to spread more bacteria and filth. Rats are the 'orcs' of the British natural landscape. Ugly, loathsome purveyors of evil. Yet, in a way, they have their purpose. They give the fox, heron, owl and buzzard something to eat.

Love them or hate them, maize crops are a huge part of the agricultural landscape here in Norfolk. The farm plan on this estate is no different. I don't mean the slender cover-crop strips raised to protect the game-birds. These are ploughed back into the land when the season is over. Energy from biomass, sent to anaerobic digesters, is a booming new industry here. Every available spare acre of land is planted with high energy-yield maize. An ugly and horizon blocking crop. Where once a man could stand and stare across the fields to watch the sunset, now he will see just tall, tatty stalks. Vermin, of course, have a bonanza when the kernels are ripe. Rabbits, deer, squirrels and badgers can all feast on a fruit never intended for human or herd consumption. The energy is in the stalks and leaves which are pulped and clamped to be fed into the digester domes as needed. I hate the maize, for its screening of once wide open vistas. I love the maize for the opportunity it gives to hunt vermin around its margins.

The rabbit warrens on Eden were (I'm reliably informed) gassed out long before I walked here. Now there are small enclaves across the estate where the conies are finding a foothold; or should that be pawhold? I'm very partial to rabbit meat so I farm these small warrens carefully. It's good to see the kits frolic on a summer afternoon but their numbers need to be kept in check in some areas.

I pull the lurcher back firmly by his collar before he sticks his curious nose into a wide hole in the woodland path. A hole with a sound emanating from within that resembles a garden strimmer. The badgers have dug out a wasps nest overnight. The angry insects are busy repairing the damage. We retreat swiftly, 'lest we get the blame!

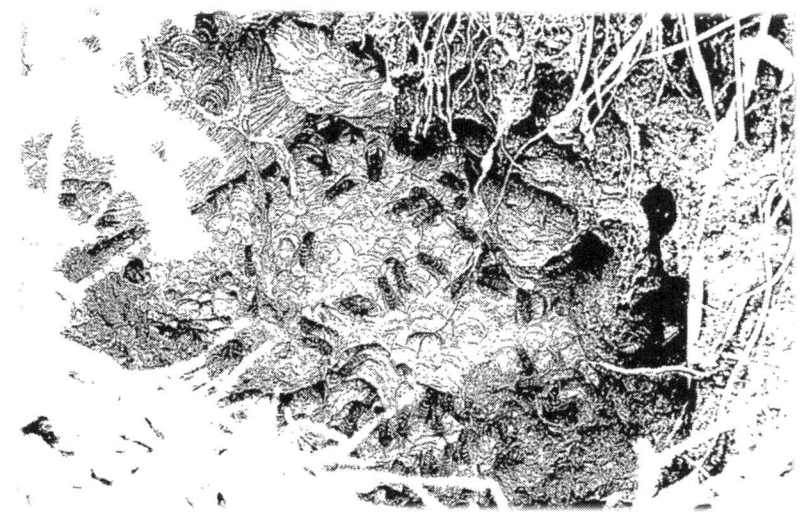

I can hear the sound of feasting amongst the bracken on the Eastern slope of the ridge overlooking the river. Stalking in silently I'm soon rewarded by the sight of a handsome roebuck. He has heard me approach and fixes me with a noble stare before barking a warning to his nearby harem and thundering off into the wood.

The hedgerow pickings are rife and ripe for gathering. Blackberry and raspberry (if you know where the best bushes are) are at their prime. Sweet chestnuts litter the forest floor, inviting collection ... a roasted evening treat or perhaps saved for the Christmas stuffing. Sloes hang heavy on the blackthorn to be used in homemade winter warmers. Apples await collection. Better used in a pie (with the blackberries) than left rotting on the floor.

Sadly I have never, ever seen a single hedgehog on Eden. Nor any evidence of one. No scats, no dead ones. Nothing. The summer rides have been riddled with thick black slugs. Perfect hedgehog territory. Or is it? With probably more than a hundred badgers in a thousand acres, the little furze-pigs are probably wise to stay away.

Just as I'm about to place a hand on a fallen trunk, I retract it swiftly, spotting what looks like a fox scat on the bark. It's not a fox turd. It is something far more ugly. A leopard slug; another of Natures perverse creations. I'm sure it's mother loves it!

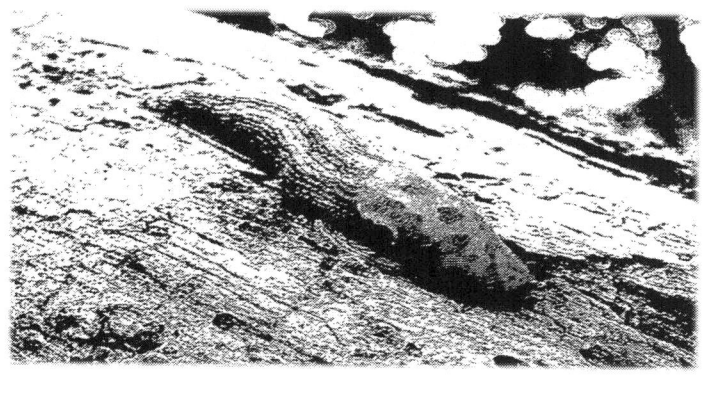

The kestrel that survived the winter famine is back over the orchard meadow again. He hovers, head down, his keen eyes focused on the movement below him. The quivering wingtips are burning energy by the kilojoule. He drops like a stone into the rye grass, lost to sight for a few seconds, then emerges with his kill.

I'm studying the birdlife out on the water meadows when a handsome dragonfly lands on the fence rail I'm leaning on. A common darter. *Sympetrum striolatum*.

The old lurcher is trotting just a few yards too many ahead of my muzzle, so I whisper him to heel. He is turning maverick in his dotage. We are approaching an open gate and track behind the White Cottage. I want him close because this is a lively spot for wildlife. The old boy is half-blind and half-deaf now, his thirteen years telling on him. He doesn't hear my whisper and blunders on. As I look along the track beyond the gate, a healthy mature rabbit is browsing at the margin. The dog's movement brings it alert. It sits up, staring at the hound but Dylan is completely oblivious to its presence. It's only ten feet from him. His nose is glued to the ground, his paw raised; a demeanour that tells me he has smelt rabbit. I despair. The coney sits obligingly so I raise the rifle but before I can fire, a hairy blur blocks the view. I look up over the gun. The rabbit has gone and my lurcher is sniffing the spot where it sat.

Strolling down a track between two tumbling flint walls my hawk-like eye (though only when I'm wearing my specs) catches a glimpse of a little creature as it darts into the shade of some ivy. I slide the camera from my bag and stand stock still, focusing on the large flint which is baking in the mid-day sun. The creature emerges again; the same blink-of-an-eye movement. A common lizard and the first I've seen here. Staring through the zoom lens, I admire its prehistoric beauty as it basks in the heat. A cloud passes over the sun and my little dinosaur disappears with the flick of a tail.

I am a hunter and there are hares here in abundance. I must have placed the cross-hairs of my scope on the witch's eye a hundred times since I started walking here. I have never pulled the trigger. I have never even disengaged the safety on my rifle. Not just because I love to watch the wild hare. Not just because of the negligible damage it does around the farm. More because I see the depth of inherited wisdom set within that knowing eye. The hare is born in the field beneath the open sky. From birth to death it will run or lope from threat and menace with a confidence in its own survival. The hare is the creature that most represents the concept of the Tao. It fears nothing and lives for the moment, not even considering its own death. It simply turns its face to the wind, makes a decision and moves away from conflict. We can learn much from the hare.

An amazing encounter! Leaving twelve-acre wood, I follow the boundary fence on a bright morning and spot a hint of tawny fur amongst the beet leaves. I hush the lurcher to heel, thinking it's a fox. The dog lies down as the animal pops its head up. It is a roe kid, feeding on the green leaves. The kid simply looks at me, chewing away as I take some snaps. Eventually it saunters further into the crop. There is no sign of the mother.

Another rare visitor from the river margins to the escarpment is the reed bunting, *Emberiza schoeniclus.* The male buntings are immediately identifiable with their sable crown, little white moustache and white collar. A dignified but furtive bird, resident all year round. They visit these woods at their peril as they are easily spotted (singing atop a shrub or low sapling) by our ruthless old friend, the sparrowhawk.

Just as I'm about to place my hand on the gatepost, I see the wasp and withdraw my palm swiftly. Yet, it's not a wasp. This huge black and yellow striped arthropod is three times the size of a wasp. This specimen is huge, even for its own species. *Vespa crabro*, a hornet. Though not as aggressive as its smaller cousin, I give it a wide berth. It still has a powerful sting, I'm told.

I'm sitting in cover watching some carrion bait I've left out for the magpies in the grassy clearing. The birdsong in this corner of the Garden Wood has been magnificent. Wood warbler, blue and long-tailed tits, chaffinch, greenfinch, song thrush, blackbird, wren and robin. Suddenly, my mind drifting as I swat away the plaguing midges, I realise that the wood has fallen silent. A deep, disturbing and palpable nothingness. I look first to the sky, wondering if a storm is imminent but that isn't the cause. A flash of swift movement draws my eyes to a sparrowhawk making a pass across the clearing before swooping upward like a fighter jet. It calls and passes again. Nothing has stirred, none have succumbed to the hawks scare tactic and it sweeps away to try some other quarter. It takes a full five minutes for the birdsong to resume.

Trekking down the North drive, I spot two roe deer trotting nose to tail. A doe and her suitor, both oblivious to the dog and I. The lurcher is following their scent, his nose firmly to the ground. His scent his last sensory bastion; all else is failing. The roebuck, when I reach within about twenty yards, stands alert to stare at me. I can't see his paramour. He barks loudly and the dog jumps a foot off the ground. The buck bolts, over the barbed wire and into the cattle pasture. The doe leaps from beneath a juniper bush and sprints into the wood. My dog returns his nose to the damp grass as though nothing has happened. What had happened was a short *interruptus* to *coitus,* I am certain.

The harvested barley still hides a multitude of protein in the form of discarded grain, enjoyed by bird and beast. Crow, hares and woodpigeon scour the stubbles for the bounty left behind by the long-departed combines. I lay a few decoy shells and add some pigeons to the bag. The perfect basis for some warm winter casseroles. Spring seed protected, an autumn harvest for the guardian, winter fodder for all. Farming and nature. Nature and hunting. Synchronistic. Symbiotic.

The pheasant is a stupid bird; have I mentioned that already? The poults that have survived the weather, worms and vermin have taken to the rides inside of staying in cover near the feeders. Their survival is far more threatened here than in the rearing pens of commercial shooting estates but at least they are free to run and fly. The birds here are truly 'free-range', wild pheasants. Coming across a nye of poults in the open today, my old lurcher helped me nudge them back into the safety of the coverts as the buzzards wheeled, disappointedly, above.

A small brownish butterfly flutters by and lights on a nettle head. The two white spots inside the 'eye' painted on each wing distinguish it from the Meadow Brown, its cousin. It is a Gatekeeper; *Pyronia tithonus*.

Before I step into the cover of the twelve-acre wood, I need to check the breeze. There are dozens of dandelion clocks on the margin. I pick one and blow it. The breeze is a Westerly. It is in my favour.

September

September is the true Autumn month. The sun sinks lower every day and the unpicked fruit starts to fall and rot. The morning dews soak the boots and the mists hang above the water meadows until the mid-morning sun finds the strength to burn them away. Perhaps the most poignant reminder that winter looms is the gathering of the swallows on the wires; then their eventual departure. Fly firmly, old friends and please bless us with your presence next summer.

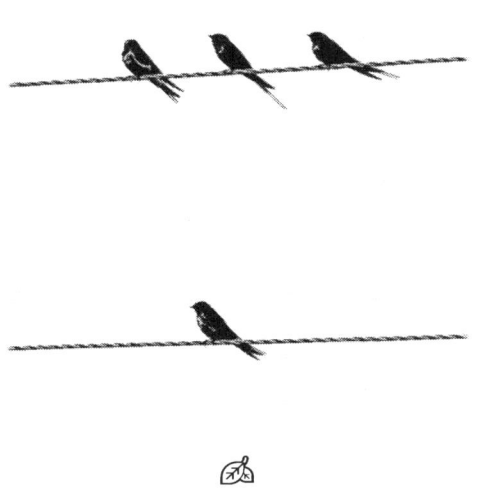

Stalking through the Escarpment Wood, the lurcher and I are troubled by hecklers. The blue tits protest at our passing. They flit and fuss out of reach, their feeble *'tsee, tsee'* is their only weapon against man and dog. Can they not remember that we removed the jackdaw that found their nest? Plucky little birds … with amnesia.

"Diddly dum, diddly dee, one for you and one for me!" The magpies and jackdaws are out on the short-cropped turf of the horse paddock at mid morning. They're dancing comically like drunken fathers and uncles at a wedding reception. Hopping from one foot to the other, chasing along the sward; Riverdance on the meadow. It's the crane-fly hatch, prompted by the warm September sun on the grass. Beneath the sods, the leather-jacket pupae have pushed out and transformed from an ugly crop-nuisance bug into the delicate, slender daddy-long-legs, *Tipula paludosa*. The birds are hunting the emerging flies. Even when they catch them, swallowing the gangly, wriggling arthropods is a challenge. Hence the chasing!

September is a time when, traditionally, I abandon Eden for a while and seek another. The family holiday. This year we indulge in the remoteness of a cottage beneath Carn Fadryn in North Wales. A tump that holds a raven roost, so yours truly is more than happy with the venue. A climb up Snowdon tests the legs and lungs of this Norfolk man to almost CPR point. Later it makes me appreciate the difference between hobbits and dwarfs. The escarpments on Eden would seem trifling for months to come.

From my stand in the covert I first hear, then see, the approach of Armageddon. I quickly test the breeze with a handful of pine pollen; my fears are confirmed. I need to get out of this place fast. I rustle up the dog and head West as swiftly as I can, though I know I can't outrun the breeze. There is nowhere on the estate today where I could be safe from this catastrophe while there is a stiff Easterly blow. Lawrence, the farmer, has drawn the septic tanks. As the small tanker spreads its load with clinical efficiency across the nether-meadow, the whole valley is swamped in the stench of human effluent. Sometimes, as they say … 'stercus accidit'!

Across on the stubbles, squadrons of woodies frustrate my hunting genes. They always seem to congregate way beyond the range of my feeble gun. Some guile is therefore needed. A few 'tools and engines of deceit'. Isn't that how the magistrates of old described the poacher's kit? No, I won't be threading horsehair through raisins to make the birds sit trying to disgorge them. Nor will I be wasting my single malt on dipping grain to intoxicate the birds. These were tricks reputedly used to disable and poach pheasants back in Richard Jeffries era. No, I will simply lay a few flocked shell decoys close to a 'sitty' tree and snipe the curious pigeons that land to take a look.

Their spiked armour fails to intimidate me, for I am armed. Today they are the enemy, the quarry, the hunted. They lurk in the treetops, hiding amongst the long, tear-drop shaped leaves. Treacherous, perilous vermin; to be shot on sight. They are the fruit of *Aesculus hippocastunum*, the horse chestnut. Ideal for practising the black art of shooting elevated targets. Today, they are pseudo-crows and I? I am Barnett the conkeror.

A flock of minuscule birds race past, stopping to take seeds from the teasel heads. Their song varies from an ugly rasp to a melodic trill. The broad bills reveal their family; finches, seed breakers. These are a charm of goldfinches, the dandies of the British field and hedge.

Great squadrons of that perpetual pest, the woodpigeon, gather in the hedgerows and trees watching the remaining barley stems being rolled into huge bales. This is their chance to plunder the last of the grain shaken from the yellow straw and who can blame them. The grain will only go to waste. Like the woodpigeons the corvids, rats and mice will help sweep the floor. For a while, the bales will lie around the fields before being collected and stacked. I have written before that they look to me like the scattered champagne corks of the gods, the morning after their harvest party.

The potato crops are being harvested. The farm technology now is amazing and the process fascinating ... but they still haven't perfected it yet, have they? One would expect (by now) that the spuds would be pulled from the ground at one end and appear at the other end of the machine as a packet of Walkers crisps or McCain's oven chips. I guess that there are still many of us left who like to peel, boil, mash or roast real potatoes? I know I certainly do.

The woodland floor is littered with dead wood, the remnants of the deforestation exercise earlier in the year. I'm stalking slowly, trying to avoid stepping on the twigs, which crack like a firework under the incautious boot. My gaze is switching from canopy to floor constantly. Just as I'm about to step over an olive coloured sprig, it moves. I step back and watch it wriggle slowly for a yard, then stop. *Anguis fragilis.* A slow worm and a small one, at only a foot and a half long. It isn't really a worm; nor is it a snake. It's a harmless, legless lizard and gorger of slugs and invertebrates. A real gardener's friend. I'm tempted to take it home but, alas, my good lady hates squirmy, wormy, snaky things.

One of the most common bankside plants is the cow parsley; *Anthriscus sylvestris*. In some areas the plants white flower gives it the nickname Queen Anne's lace. Few people realise that it is a member of the carrot family.

The swallows are still congregating on the wires, preparing to depart their summer haunts. Where did the birds gather before telegraphy, I wonder? The vast distance they will cover on their flight to the Southern Hemisphere bends the mind of a man who rarely leaves his beloved Norfolk. We are blessed that these athletic little midge-hawkers choose our fields for half the year. It's said that should you see a swallow fly between the legs of a farm beast, bad luck will ensue. I would guess that you'll probably get wet. Low flying swallows, like swifts, are often the harbinger of a storm as they follow the insects being driven down by the weather front.

A glorious autumn morning and along the dew sodden forest rides I find myself side-stepping hundreds of black slugs. They are crawling from sunlight to shade, seeking sanctuary. Far be it from me to criticise Mother Nature's plan, which has a place and purpose for everything, but is there any creature more loathsome to the sight than a slug? Their purpose, of course (if you discount the horrendous damage they do to the vegetable patch and plant borders) is as one of Natures organic cleaners. They hoover up detritus and rot on the woodland floor. They also feed the badger and the fox (which is why, I suspect, the opportunity of a rabbit kit or pheasant poult is far more attractive!).

A cold touch on the nape of my neck, like a poke from Lucifer, makes me reach behind defensively. The creature is difficult to grasp and remove. *Lipoptena cervi ;* the deer ked. The fourth I've pulled from my flesh this morning and my neck will itch and tingle until I shower later. The keds attack is suicidal, kamikaze. Having found its host, it casts its wings. I study it closely. An ugly, tiny arachnid and too much like a tick for my liking. I flick it away. Without wings, its life will be short … yet its legacy is ancient. Remains of deer keds were found on the Stone Age mummy, *Otzi* when he was uncovered in 1991. Thus keds are at least four thousand years old and still seeking human blood.

A slick and stealthy jink of rufus fur catches my eye. A snaking, belly-to-the-floor exploration of the floor. I'm sitting in the Garden Wood intercepting squirrels as they traverse between bough and bird table. The creature stops suddenly and sits up, scenting an atmosphere drenched in the scent of pine sap and rotting bracken. One of the estates most voracious predators suspects that I am here, but isn't sure. An admirable foe. Ruthless in its predation of young game birds and my Sunday stew, the rabbits. Much as I love watching them hunt, I have never been able to 'sex' a stoat until I've shot it. This was a dog stoat.

The fruit of the rowan tree (or mountain ash) is often held to be an indicator of impending winter conditions. The trees hang heavy with the bright red fruit this year. Some country folk will be saying a harsh winter looms. Yet they were stacked with fruit last year and we had one of the mildest winters I've experienced in my sixty years.

This is the month of the woodpigeon. Huge flocks gather again, as they did in spring to raid the seedlings. This time they are cleaning up the spilt grain left on the open fields after the harvest. A harmless occupation (but an opportunity to fill my freezer). Watch them for a while, they are admirable birds; skilled in flight and amazingly agile in the air.

Along the manicured rides, the autumn sun sends down shimmering spotlights. They illuminate the slow cascade of leaf-fall, displaced by a gentle zephyr. The heat is overbearing, so the breeze is welcome. An Indian summer is upon us. I blow a ked from my wrist, before it can draw blood. Walking below a sycamore, a gust of warm wind sends down a shower of tiny whirligigs. The descending seeds surround me, a helicopter attack. I surrender in blissful wonder. Nature is such a magical entertainer.

Two days of violent storms and torrential rain have impacted on Eden. Sprigs of oak and beech litter the drives as I motor in. I have to stop and remove a heavy branch from the track. Walking the newly mown rides which David has recently revived, I find myself kicking the storm litter away. Out on the 'pap-meadow' where the cess-pit effluent is spread, I see a fallen birch tree on the neighbour's border and walk across to inspect it. A tree under which I often paused by the wire to watch the hares and buzzards. The trunk is blackened and burned in places. A lightning strike victim.

Climbing from the Garden Wood to the escarpment I follow the edge of the stubbles up to the old, abandoned orchard. The apple trees here still thrive and today the boughs are heavy with ripe, green 'cookers'. I look about, furtively. Suddenly, I'm eleven years old again instead of nearly sixty. I open my game-bag and fill it with fruit. The blackberries along the hedgerow are ripe too, so I fill one of the small bags I keep to carry squirrel tails. Apple and blackberry crumble, naturally harvested, beckons. When I was ten to thirteen years old we were often caught and censured for such harvesting or seen running into the distance with our spoils. Scrumping, we called it then. It had a wicked romanticism to it … like rabbit poaching. The real crime, I realise now, is to leave such bounty rotting on the floor.

Today, I am the self appointed marshal of the pheasant feeders. Almost every one I have passed has been nudged over by either deer or badgers. I suspect it's the badgers, as I like to blame the badgers for everything wrong around here. They are just subterranean hooligans.

Thursday, September 22nd, 2016 and a milestone for me as it's my sixtieth birthday. Three score years. Hopefully with the biblical ten to go (at least!). Everyone else is working so I decamp to Eden. I even leave old Dylan behind, determined to have a self-indulgent session on the woodpigeons. My new rifle is a Special Edition stamped number 60 (of 100) in honour of the occasion. A birthday present to me, for only a shooter would understand the bond between hunter and gun. I head across to the old marl pit which stands in a knell above the cattle pasture. I have a natural hide crafted there where I have harvested hundreds of woodies. It is a natural oasis for passing birds. When I climb down into the pit, I am shocked. A middle-aged and ivy-strangled oak has snapped half way up its trunk and swamped my hide in timber and evergreen. There, but for the grace of God ...! For a few minutes, I reflect on the accuracy of the tree-fall. I must have angered the god of woodpigeons. I look about. The trunks topple has opened up a whole new vista and, in itself, formed a new opportunity for a better hide. Another, unexpected, birthday present.

On the North drive I see the fallow herd again ... or at least, part of it. Six hinds and a young hart. He has barely a show of his first antlers coming through. They sense me, mill about then trot into the garden wood.

The morning mist has coated the spider's web with moisture; the September sun illuminates the pure artistry of the arachnid architecture. The spider sits in the centre of its gossamer net, waiting for the slightest quiver that might indicate a catch.

The cock pheasant struts on the turf of the North drive, dressed in all his finery. A striking beau, for sure. Alas, he is unaware that the close season will fall with tonight's lowering sun. He will be fairly safe here, for a while, if he keeps his head down and stops his promenading.

October

Is October the last month of autumn … or the first month of winter? I'm never quite sure. To me, it is the month of the fungal bloom and the howling gale. In Eden, both are spectacular. To stand on the escarpment midst the mighty, ancient trunks and watch them bend in a fierce blow is like standing with Tolkien's 'Ents'. The trees talk to each other. It's like listening to an old vinyl record slowed down. I can only imagine what they're saying to each other. *"Hold fast, old Elm. It will pass!"* *"Clench the roots, Beech, my friend. Get a grip!"* While down in the lower woods, amid the moss and mulch, the fragile fungi creep forth. The fifth natural kingdom. Their mycelium gather and feed on the host of wood, leaf or detritus. Only when they need to reproduce does the toadstool, mushroom or other three dimensional forms appear, fed from the hyphae beneath. It's only function is to develop, protect and disperse the spores that spread the species.

I stand on the escarpment staring North across the tranquil patchwork tapestry of the river valley. A skein of Canada's wheel in from the West, all flap and clamour. They descend to the cattle pasture and add black-feathered texture to a green landscape already flecked with the white of mute swan and egret. The breeze in my face has a keen edge to it. Somewhere out in the North Sea an Arctic-born blow is building. Boughs will bend and creak tonight.

An unusual crop of fungi is attacking a discarded pine log. The ultimate indignity for a piece of wood cut by the foresters and discarded as surplus to requirements. The fungi is Oyster Rollrim; *Tapinella panuoides*.

An early morning sortie, avoiding the game feeders. The birds are dogged in and deep in cover, close to the recycled curry powder barrels. Best I don't disturb them. They need to relax for they will run the gauntlet soon. As always, I avoid the fields and coverts on the shoot days of the pheasant season. My work has been trifling in the protection of the poults, yet I guess some find it useful. A succession of crows and squirrels have fallen to the popgun through the spring and summer, protecting nest and poult. For me, however, it is the unexpected song of the rising skylark on this October morning that speaks success rather than the muted salvo of the first guns; or the crow of the startled ring-necked cock.

On a breezy October morning the patter of the dry, falling leaves is incessant; like the sound of a summer shower.

There is a stranded, spectacular beech tree in the crop field outside the twelve-acre wood. Sometimes it has pigeons and crows for company. Occasionally a deer may lie at its feet or pheasants may huddle down amongst the nettles that surround it in high summer. The Meadow Witch will find shade there on hot, humid days. I rest beneath it often; to shelter from summer rain or to set a hide and decoy the autumn woodies. A fine tree, full of stature and purpose.

A rustle above lifts my eyes. Up in the pendunculate oak, the leaves appear to wrestle each other before parting to reveal a grey harvester. A half-ripe pair of acorns tumble into the mulch between my boots. There was a time ... I would have been in nappies ... when the native red squirrel blessed these woods. *Sciurus vulgaris,* the wood sprite. Now beaten into retreat from most British treescapes by the grey squirrel, *Sciurus Carolinensis.*

The Indian Summer sunshine strikes a hatch. The wood and meadow erupt into an entomologists Nirvana; all hover and buzz. I tread the dew-sodden turf of the pasture and clouds of yellow dung-flies lift from the fresh cow-pats. They circle and return again to feed. I love their Latin name, *Scatophaga stercoraria*; which literally means shit-eaters! They will endure in the meadows until the hoar-frosts come.

Returning to the motor one morning I spot what looks like a white football sitting in the shrubs near the Hall. Curious, I investigate and find it's a giant puffball; *Langermannia gigontea*. It is larger than my boot ... but, alas, the flesh is too mature to be eaten.

Out along the track between the farm and the twelve-acre wood, I follow the straight line trail of a fox, its pad prints clearly outlined in the wet mud. A purposeful trot, no meandering, straight to the coverts. The fox print is distinctive; the pads are covered in fur so each hair shows clearly. The claws are retracted, demonstrating passive travel rather than stalking (when the claws will be flexed).

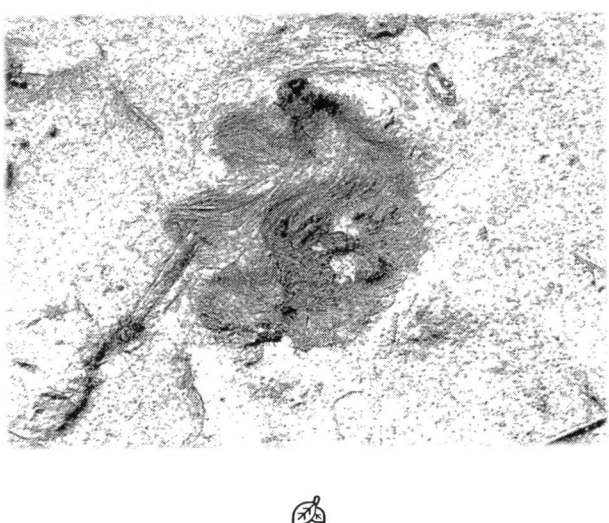

Along the forest floor, amid the leaf mulch, I see what appear to be two large eyeballs staring up at the moulting branches. Have I stumbled on a dead Minion? No, it's just a pair of shaggy parasol mushrooms.

The lurchers damp nostrils are flaring but he's reluctant to advance. He can smell her, but knows that she and I have history. He looks to me for a prompt, which I deny. In the crepuscular gloom of the copse I can see her staring at me. She can't see the dog but she and I can see each other clearly across the dying bracken. Perhaps our twentieth stand-off in the last five years? The Witch of the wood invites her own death by lingering long enough for me to raise the rifle scope. I stare into her eye at six-time magnification. Her eye is the mirror of my soul. She knows it. To dull that wild glint would shatter my own ferality. Blinkless, the she-hare lopes languidly towards the woods margin. There are times to kill and there are times to appreciate the few truly wild souls that walk the world with us. The dog looks to me with an air of understanding, his own chestnut eyes swimming with primitive wisdom. The eye of the legendary hound, Gelert. The wisdom of the dogs that hunted alongside kings and princes in the ancient forests before we wrecked the land for vanity and profit.

Yet another Indian summer morn and we're blessed with sunshine. We walk, the hound and I, out to Pine Wood. So named due to the high pines, *Pinus sylvestris*, which line the central ride. The trek to the wood is exposed. Just a few spinnied oaks and a stand of maize shelter our progress. The blue, cloudless sky is a green-screen for the wheeling rooks as they harass an old buzzard benignly soaring on the thermals. The rooks eventually win. The oldest raptor in the valley retreats again. Not with ignominy. Definitely not through fear. He floats away with the resignation of a husband avoiding a nagging wife.

The carpet of sweet chestnut kernels on the woodland floor is a minefield for my tender-pawed lurcher. He hops about like a failed fire-walker. However, they make great natural targets for shooting practise, so revenge is exacted accordingly. I swear the dog wants to cheer every time I shoot one from a fence post.

The constant trickle of rustic leaf-fall resembles an orange / brown snowstorm. The lurcher lies on the damp mulch as I scour the canopy for mammalian movement. Every leaf that drops tickles the senses. Hairs tremble and nostrils flare. Ears rotate like radar dishes and eyes flash left and right, up and down. The dog does the same.

In the garden wood, I watch like a voyeur. Close to the wall, she browses on beechmast. She turns her back to me and her white rump looks flagrant, inviting. Least, it would were I her buck. The doe feeds, undisturbed, until a tractor rattles down the nearby track between two flint walls. Its two tines are spiked with huge silage bales for the cattle on the water meadow. She watches the machine descend for a while then slips away into anonymity.

One of the most striking species of fungi on Eden has to be the Parasol mushroom; *Macrolepiota procera*. I found a specimen today so huge, I laid my rifle alongside it to illustrate its size. Parasols are highly edible but must definitely be cooked. I can't, though, bring myself to harvest this monster. It deserves to stand untouched.

I stand in the twelve-acre wood appalled at the vandalism spread out before me. The trash and spread of cut timber offends me. The scent of pine sap hangs in the air like the stench of blood over a battlefield. I can feel my heartbeat rise. The wood has been raped. I take deep breaths and inhale 'reason'. This is not my wood. It is a crop and it has just been garnered. Such a harvest as happens only twice in a mans lifetime. The dog and I pick our way carefully across the detritus like beachcombers. Not a mammal stirs. Not a corvid rattles. There were wood-hares here! They are far from here now. Philip, the master carpenter, hails me when I return to the car. He crafts such beauty here, in the heart of the estate. An artisan and a gentleman. He fusses the lurcher and the dog fusses him. We yarn for a while, both aching at the ravishment of the nearby forest. Yet, we both understand. He needs wood for his own craft. I need the forest for mine. Out of the old, will come new.

I stop in my tracks to claw the camera from my bag. On a fallen stump overhanging the brook, a cluster of ochre fungi cling precariously to the bark. Elvish steps leading down to the bubbling stream. This must be where the sprites and nymphs climb down to wash their sylvan robes? Or have I been reading too much Tolkien? The fungus is sulphur-tuft.

The first hints of the impending gale creep across this flat Norfolk landscape like the tendrils of an invasive weed. A gust here, a sharp breeze there ... until the sound turns gradually from whisper to call. From call to rant. From rant to rage. The trees start to bend and creak, shedding the last of the clinging leaves. Watching the canopy stripped bare is like watching a time-lapse film of maggots stripping a dead corpse. At its height, the fury of the wind storm shouts "change!" and uproots the weak, topples the brittle, levels the dead. Even the healthy ... the gargantuan beech and the ancient oak ... take injury, losing bough and limb. When it's all over, I walk the wood and marvel at Natures cleansing. Dead brash litters the floor. Above and around, the strongest have survived.

Is there any bird that enjoys the gale more than our humble rook, '*Corvus frugilegus*'? The wind-dancer. Watching the black throng challenging the gale today is like watching dolphins cavort in a rolling tide. The birds float with the wind then turn into the jet-stream, primary feathers spread to catch the flow. Hovering for a while, the birds fight the draught then tumble and wheel, recovering before they hit the ground. All the while, there is a glorious rook-shout in the air. A celebration of skill and flight-fuelled freedom. A child's scream in a water-chute. A raised fist and cry of joy at the referees whistle. The rooks spit in the eye of Natures fury then beat away, en-masse, towards some distant night-time roost. The gale, insulted, cranks up it wrath another notch.

The stench of progressive agriculture fills the afternoon air. The 'Terragators' are abroad in nearby fields, spreading muck and spoil. Drilling it into the nitrogen deficient soil to feed the next rotational crop of choice. The cloying scent lies putrid under the evening mist. Even the lurcher closes his curious nostrils, curls his tail and seeks sanctuary indoors. Later, on his bed behind the sofa later, he farts. The irony, not lost on me, is lost on him.

"Jay, squirrel, squirrel, jay? Who will plant the oak today?" Not a quote, sorry. I just made it up. The competition in the canopy for the oak-fruit is full-on now. Both grey squirrel and jay are picking off the acorns and carrying them away to cache them for winter sustenance. Both bury the acorns and it seems random in both species. How do they remember where they have hidden the fruit? Often, of course, they don't. They will forget and so a new seed is planted. The acorn may become a sapling. The sapling, a mighty oak. In twenty years time, the jay and the squirrel will compete again in the new tree and new forest. *"Jay, squirrel, squirrel, jay? Who will plant the oak today?"*

October is the month of fungal bloom. Trails of unseen mycelium crawl across a perfect blend of moist and rotting mulch or decomposing tree. They accumulate into a rise of disparate and three dimensional monuments to Natures glory. A spectacle of colour, craft, shape and texture. Parasols, brackets, toadstools, mushrooms and puff-balls. Boletes, wax-caps, brittle-gills and poisonpies. Chanterelles, milk-caps, web-caps and bonnets. Some are edible, others best left untouched. One of my favourites, the fly-agaric, is one of the earliest bloomers. Red for danger. Be warned!

Even the most reluctant of the leaves are detached now; the canopy above skeletal and naked. The comforting tramp of Vibram sole on a luxurious russet carpet allows for stealthy progress across the forest floor. Recklessly, I celebrate and kick a pile of oak leaves into the air. The winning conversion in a hard fought match. The old lurcher jumps in alarm and jinks away thinking he has done something wrong. I kick another clump lightly towards him and the dog realises it's a game. He sprints in to bury his muzzle in the mulch then lifts it, showering me with leaf mould. He barks in puppyish play and I hush him quickly. The game is over already. His opening-up will warn too many that we're here. We resume our sombre stalk and dignity prevails.

The forest floor is littered with sweet chestnuts after some squally days. I set about filling a carrier bag with this autumn bounty. There is an easy, painless way of harvesting the nuts from their spiked armour without touching the barbs. Simply roll the ripe kernels under your boot and they will split, spilling the nuts. Back at home, wash the chestnuts, discard any with small holes in them; there will be weevils in these. Using a sharp knife, cut a cross on the flatter side of the nuts, spread them on a baking tray and roast them for half an hour in an oven pre-heated to 200^0C. A delicious winter evening snack.

Out near twelve-acre wood I watch another jay labour across the meadow with it's distinctive bobbing flight. It's carrying an acorn, the slender stalk dangling from its broad bill. The journey looks perilous. One false move and the acorn could drop to be lost in the meadow forever … and many are.

> *"One for the larder or one for the wood?*
> *Food for the jay, or another oak stood?"*

We've all done it. Admit it! Plucked the dusty black fruit of the blackthorn and popped it in our mouth? That sickly bitter sloe, spat out in clear regret! A useful berry, much loved by an eclectic collection of birds; gathered by the gin and jam maker. A false grape on a barbarous vine.

The stench of carrion in the beech grove assails my olfactory senses. Yet the dog ignores the scent. Strange? He rarely passes up the chance to roll on a rotting corpse. It's a wild dog thing ... hyenas and Cape hunting dogs do it to disguise their own scent. The source of the odour, I soon find, is a trio of stinkhorn fungi, *Phallus impudicus*. Translated from the Latin this means 'shamelessly phallic'. The stench is caused by the olive green 'gleba', a slime that covers the cap. This attracts insects like bluebottles, which pick up the gel (therefore the fungal spores) on their feet and spread them. Another example of Natures ingenuity. It was said that the Victorian gardeners and gamekeepers used to knock these stinkhorns over with their sticks each morning, lest they excited 'impressionable' young ladies walking in the grounds.

Along the woodland floor I catch sight of another crimson speckled beauty, in perfect form. A stunning example of its genus. I want to pick it up and caress it, smell it. Like a red rose bud. Yet I don't. It is a fly agaric fungus. *Amanita muscaria*. A scarlet poisoner. A destroyer of sanity.

The carrot-boys are here to put the carrots to bed. I can tell by all the muck and slosh. Co-operative farming at its best. I don't know how they do it but whatever they're planting (I call it Agent Orange) will be hidden under a blanket of straw to keep off the frosts. In about ten weeks time they'll be back, pulling up thousands of the orange vegetables in time for our Christmas dinners. With the straw down, you never even see a green carrot-top. Perhaps another reason the rabbits are scarce here?

Along the escarpment I chance across an avalanche of honey fungus clinging to the exposed roots at the base of a birch tree. *Armillaria mellea.* Though it is stunning to look at, this isn't healthy for the tree. This is a fungus which attacks the living as well as the dead. If the lace-like rhizomorphs from which the fungal fruit evolve attack the root system, the tree may die. Nor is it a fussy foe in the forest. It will attack both coniferous and deciduous trees and nothing can stop it.

I am in no way 'religious'. Yet I believe in the concept of the Tao. I read the Tao Te Ching many years ago. A philosophy scribed by Lao Tzu long before it was adopted by Buddhists and twisted into a 'religion'. Lao Tzu's own writings decry the concept of 'religion'. The work is simply an appraisal of the natural order. We come from a force which we will never understand. We contribute to its need, either positively or negatively. Then we go back to it in death. October is the month to appreciate that philosophy. The fungi season. Out of death and decay becomes life. The colourful and varied display of the fungi bloom is powerful in its presence. A perfect example of the cycle of the Tao, which many of us simply call 'Mother Nature'.

Stalking amidst the escarpment trees, I hear a sound reminiscent of a breaking wave on a stormy shore. A hundred or so woodpigeon have erupted from the woodland floor on sensing my approach. They were feeding on the beech mast littering the damp, autumn leaf mulch.

Overhead, on this splendid sun-blessed morning, the crows are complaining. Rook-shout and jackdaw chatter fills the air beyond the moulting canopy. Why do they protest so? Is it because the gales have yet to clear the last of the clinging leaves and declare it 'winter'? Perhaps the buzzard is aloft and in their airspace? Has the farmer been sloth in turning the plough and lifting the leather-jackets? Who truly knows why the crows are grumbling yet again upon the wing. It's a crow thing.

November

There are magpies gossiping like fish-wives in the ivy at the edge of the wood. It's too late in the year for it to be family group. During the winter, *'pica pica'* family groups knit together with others and put aside their territorial summer behaviour; an avian Mafia. Today, I count eighteen brigands hopping from tree to tree. This is Natures way of ensuring that youngsters pair off healthily during the cold season and avoid in-breeding. They will be amongst the first birds to nest and breed next spring, therefore a danger to songbirds and poults. *"One for sorrow, two for joy"?* ... I think not.

A full moon still hangs high in the morning blue; lingering like the last guest to leave a dinner party. The chill breeze scrapes my glow-red cheeks as I stomp along the track to the twelve-acre wood. To starboard, two huge white wind-turbines wave their ugly arms in silent disruption. I stand, like Don Quixote, to challenge this vandalism of a rural horizon; and fail. Yet such is 'progress'. Ahead, the lurcher's breath rises in a mist above his lolling tongue. He stops to sniff at a badger bog and I usher him away. TB, or not TB? That is the question.

Beyond the full-moon I creep along the rides with close intent. Not for me the claim to 'left and right', though I admire those who achieve it. Not for me the pin-feather to push into my cap. The woodcock have arrived. Although their haunts are noted, year on year, they never fail to make my heart leap at their sudden flight; the sound of leather slapped across a naked thigh. The birds shelter at the base of the escarpment here while the Easterlies prevail. When the North winds strike with their Siberian chill, the woodcocks move into the higher coverts. Their camouflage is amongst the finest in Nature so they sit tight unless pressed. I will walk past many more than I will see this winter.

A huge and magnificent specimen of chicken-of-the-wood fungi clings to the bark of a tree in the garden wood. *Laetiporus sulphureus* is edible in its fresh form but its flesh is not to my taste. The chicken stays in its coop today.

As a hunter, I am also a tracker. It's not just wildlife sign that catches the eye on Eden. Just as David, the deer stalker, knows the print of my boot I know his too. We both know the prints of the Lady, the gardener and others. Strange prints will invite enquiry and curiosity. Today's plethora of sign in the mud by the brook didn't worry me at all. Hoof prints with both boot and hound prints alongside. The North Norfolk Harriers have been through. The Meadow Witch and Wood Witch will have vacated the valley at the first inkling of hound-song. Not that they should worry; the Harriers are drag-hunting. Sadly, the pursuit of hares with dogs (one of the most ancient of hunting pursuits) is illegal … as I write.

In the Garden Wood, an old toppled beech has been left dismembered and redundant for years. Segmented in another Norfolk Chainsaw Massacre. It is host to a magnificent display of Artists Bracket fungi, *Ganoderma applanatum*. The fungus is named for its underside, which resembles a painter's canvas. I smile at the irony. An artist's canvas sculpted on the flat plane of a wasted bole. Would the artist have painted a study of the magnificent tree that once stood here?

Late morning on a dank November Sunday and the sudden onset of pure quiet is cloying. Not a whisper of breeze, not the subtle stir of the fragile leaf. The birdsong has stopped. The world is ending. The lurcher stands at my heel, his ears drawn back. He, too, deafened by the silence. Then we hear it. A distant, creeping patter … as though a thousand mice are running towards us. The volume increases and a staccato drumming climbs the escarpment, the percussion casting a curtain before it. The shower becomes a downpour and before we reach the sanctuary of the motor, an icy deluge. In the comfort of the 4x4, I hunt on the iPod for a rock track. I fire up the engine, turn up the blower to defrost the windows, crank up the volume and hit the 'play' button. The opening piano chords of November Rain, by Guns N' Roses, tickle through the speakers. A glance in the rear-view mirror shows a sodden lurcher with an expression that reads "Oh … how predictable!"

Spread across a decaying tree stump is a handsome fungus, Polyporus squamosus. Dryads Saddle. Its surface resembles a brush-painted copy of a hen pheasant's plumage. Dryads were tree nymphs in Greek mythology and someone imagined them using such a fungus as a saddle. But upon what? I imagine that this specimen would mount perfectly on the back of a hare. The perfect steed for a red squirrel knight on his Crusade against the grey infidel.

Many wild species are classified and named by 'association'. The bee orchid, the hornet moth and the peacock butterfly are all examples. They look similar to something else. None more so than the Hoof Fungus; *Fomes fomentarius*. Perhaps more of a donkeys hoof than a thoroughbred racehorse ... but definitely a hoof.

There is a little-used chapel in the heart of the estate, with its own small burial ground. The names on the gravestones mean little to me, but the dates do. So many fore-shortened lives; so sad. A peacock, dripping in azure plumage, stands atop one of the memorials crowing at my intrusion. Guarding the departed in a glorious, colourful splendour. I pray that those who left us so early lived their short lives to the full.

This is a time of risk for the younger trees. The grey squirrels are getting hungry and as their resources decline, they take to ring-barking. They tear away the bark of saplings to reach the nutrients in the softer pith of the inner trunk. These open wounds can kill a sapling. If the squirrels strip the bark right around, the tree will die. The conduit for photosynthesis is broken. At best, a scarred tree may survive but its timber will become twisted and gnarled; therefore useless to the forester.

The lordly beeches stand like naked, muscled warriors against the November tempest. Boles groan and boughs creak as though they are rallying each other. It is their deeply thrown roots and the pliancy of their timber which saves them. People should be like beech trees. Loyally rooted, strong, yet able to yield and let life's storms pass by.

Grey squirrels generally breed twice a year. The mating chases in the cold November wood make the rodents highly visible and therefore very vulnerable. The cold weather doesn't temper their ardour and they seem totally distracted. If they survive my attention, the kits will be born in late January to February. They, themselves, will be mating by early summer. A fecund and unstoppable tide of vermin.

I'm banned, temporarily, from my own shooting permissions for a few days during the winter. The Barbour and the gaiters have been donned. Shotguns that have sat idle for eight months are dusted off. Barrels are cleaned and stocks are oiled. Lubricated guns … but rusty dogs and rusty shooters appear from nowhere to uphold the time-honoured ritual of the pheasant season. Family and friends are press-ganged into beating. Pegs have mysteriously appeared in fields and on the valley slopes. The shotgun and the driven shoot are not my 'bag', if you'll excuse the pun. Yet it gives great sport and pleasure to many and underpins a whole industry in this fair land. It also creates a need for the amateur vermin controller like me. Long may it continue.

Like a dank, dribbling veil draped across copse and hedgerow it creeps ever on. The sound of dawn is muted by the fog. Only the harsh call of the crow and the drip, drip, drip from the sodden bough is heard. A dark shape looms up, stepping from the scentless fugue. The roebuck sees me and bolts back behind the sylvan curtain with a bark.

A heart-breaking moment. The huge old pine up on the escarpment has toppled, breaking off half way up. Whether through disease, age or lightning I will never know. The trees cones were the size of my hand. Another familiar old friend gone but I have one of those cones on my study shelf as a memorial.

A pit-stop for hot, peppered tomato soup beneath a fallen pine trunk on a freezing morning. I lay a brace of rabbits on the floor and the lurcher lies beside them. As I sup, through my steamed spectacles I notice the dog sit up, into a squat. He is alert, bristling. I watch as a weasel circles my makeshift dining-room. The lurcher sits tight, his head tilted; his curiosity pose. The tiny mustelid *(Mustela nivalis)* has caught the scent of fresh coney blood and is following her nose, not eyes. Ten feet from the rabbits she pauses and sits up. Her coal-black eyes are wide, her whiskers shimmering. The weasel either sees or scents us and disappears in the blink of an eye beneath the blanket of rotting leaf mulch.

From the cover of the beech grove I watch the late afternoon gathering of the rooks. This late in the year, they have abandoned the rookery, which is simply a nursery. During winter, many rookeries combine to roost together. Winter rook roosts can become huge in numbers. This one, based in a swathe of high poplars further down the river valley, hosts some two or three thousand birds. What I'm watching, though, is the pre-roost ritual. The congregation. The local rooks descend en-masse on the field between the beech grove and twelve-acre wood. They chatter and shout as they float down and mill about. Slowly, the stubbles become a moving carpet of black feather. Then, before the sun sets, the black throng takes to the sky in a raucous whirlwind, beating away across the fields towards the poplars. A wonderful spectacle.

A high pitched rasping in the garden wood announces the presence of a small flock of redwings; they are picking their way through the trees, searching for holly and rowan berries. Delightful, small thrushes that migrate from Scandinavia to winter here in large numbers.

December

Where is the snow these days? These temperate winters bear no joy for me. The knee-depth trudge of boot and leg through virgin snow was a 'given' in my boyhood. Just five decades ago; don't laugh? Just five decades ago when I was ten I can remember my father having to set forth and meet my mother along paths set two feet deep with snow and drifting. A boy left 'home alone' with is eight year old sister. Both pairs of eyes glued to the cold, steel-framed windows awaiting their safe return. They burst through the door and stepped through, stamping boots and shaking snow from their hats and coats, laughing. A happy memory from my childhood. Where, now, is the December snow?

My hunter's eye catches a familiar silhouette at the edge of the wood. A roebuck is watching me intently. Most folk would have mistaken the form for a bush or fallen tree. Only when I stop to return the stare does the buck move away. Immobility is tremendous defence for many wild creatures but they know (once they're seen) it's time to flee.

Those carrot-boys are back to take up the crop. The machines lift, sort, cut off the leaves and spill the vegetables into waiting trailers. They're shipped off to a store somewhere. From soil to supermarket shelf in ten weeks. Clever agriculture. Just-In-Time agriculture. There are enough of the carrots spilled for me to grab a game-bag full. I wonder if carrot-poaching is a transportable offence? I hope so. I've always fancied a free trip to Australia.

Across Christmas I once again ban myself from the coverts and feeders. The traditional Boxing Day shoots are imminent so my presence is disruptive to the birds. They need to be close to the feeders.

The rot-down is underway. The combination of rain, hoar frosts, sun and fungal mycelium break down the leaf mulch of the forest and the stubbles on the field. The decomposition feeds the earth, returning vital nutrients to fuel the buried seed when spring arrives. This is Mother Natures work. This is the Tao. It needs no help from man. It happened before we existed and it will happen when we're gone.

Growing on top of stump in a pile of cut timber, the bright orange honey fungus stands out like beacon. It lends colour and cadence to an otherwise damp and dismal wood today. I decide I like honey fungus. It has brought a smile to my face.

The late planted sugar beet crop is ripe and in full leaf. The fields look like the canopies of lush miniature forests. They hide a myriad secrets. Frenchmen hide amongst the straight rows; safe here from the guns until Boxing Day. Then those red-legs may be stretched a tad as the tapping sticks of friends and family beat the crop (excuse the unintended pun). They will be safe if they keep running. Their only threat is in taking flight, into the path of the waiting guns. The Meadow Witch will be huddled in the beet too; a hares haven with nourishment at every turn. Her progeny will be nibbling at the sweet beet tubers but there is plenty for all, so their plunder is negligible. As I circumvent the crop, down near the brook, a pair of rufus ears catch my eye. In total contrast to the verdant green leaves of the beet. The fox, of course, thinks it's hidden. The camera is a poor excuse for the gun but the shot is taken anyway.

As I lean on the rickety wooden gate, staring out across the flood meadows, a haunting sound bears down the valley. A large flock appears, jinking and twisting in perfect unison. As fluid as a murmuration of starlings … but these birds are larger. Their call is their giveaway. The whistling wigeon lift en-masse then plunge down into a wide pool. As their webbed feet hits the surface there is a foaming explosion of flood water.

Crouched beneath an ivy-break, disguised and innocuous, I'm ready for the incoming woodies. When they alight, they won't even know I'm here. I have been meticulous in my choice of hide-out. Or so I think. A cock robin appears, with full scarlet waistcoat; a Christmas cliché. He seems to be upset at my intrusion and flits about, 'chitting' his disapproval. As he fusses around me, the first pigeons arrive. Alerted by the robin's aggression, they depart as swiftly as they arrived. Still the robin persists in his nagging. I gather up my bag and move on to find a spot without a feathered guardian. "Who killed cock robin?" Not me, honestly … but he came bloody close to it!

Down in the garden wood the roman, holly and hawthorn berries are under attack. The rasping chatter of the fruit thieves, though unseen, exposes their identity. Fieldfares. They leave their Scandinavian breeding grounds once the rowan berries have been decimated, then fly across to feed on ours. They are resilient birds, often seen feeding on the coldest days when native species are huddled at roost. While it's good to see them I know that when they've gone, spring is close.

A huge flock of birds, a maelstrom of feather, swirls in the air above the water meadow for minutes. Knots, hundreds of them. Suddenly the flock descends; it looks like someone spreading a blanket on the wet grass.

A mute swan in flight is magnificent spectacle. The powerful beat of the wide-stretched wings have to sustain enough power and speed to ensure the neck stays straight. That they migrate many thousands of miles is testament to their flying skill. It's the take-offs and landings that give them a problem!

A dawn sortie through the twelve-acre wood on a foggy pre-Christmas morning. Sunrise at this time of year being an hour after the local children have started lessons! Through the fugue, I sense movement and stand still. My scent is shrouded by the curtain of dank moisture. There are deer browsing ahead of me. They slip into the greyness like wraiths. Then my heart is nearly stopped by the unleashing of a blood-curdling scream nearby. I take a deep breath and as I relax, the banshee wails again. An unearthly sound. I stalk towards its source. Through the swirling fog I see the disappearing brush of the vixen. The rank scent of fox musk hangs in the air. The banshee, now in heat, is advertising for a mate; her shriek is her love song.

The winter die-back has reveals yet another hidden treasure on Eden. Returning to the car I cut through the artist's yard. A hut with a simple forge where a very talented lady produces iron sculptures from discarded scrap. Passing the hut I see an old iron cartwheel lying rusting against the wooden wall. Another reminder of a bygone age. The hole in its centre reminds me of the Tao Te Ching. Lao Tzu, its author, reflected that sometimes it is the 'emptiness' that gives most value. That hole in the centre of the cartwheel is empty, yet without it being so an axle could not be fitted. The inside of a clay pot is empty, yet it is that emptiness which gives it value as a vessel for storage or for cooking food.

Oh look! It's January 1st; New Years Day! Another year has turned around and left me blessed with memories, sights, sounds and knowledge. What surprises will Eden bring me this year?

The author, with Dylan, his lurcher.

Acknowledgements

I would like to take this opportunity to thank everyone involved in maintaining 'Eden'. The Lady, old Ralph the gardener, young David from the village, Lawrence the farmer and Olly, the farm manager. Thanks too to David, the deer-stalker, for introducing me to Eden and getting me permission to shoot here.

About The Author

Ian Barnett is a freelance country sports writer and photographer based in Norfolk, UK. Ian has hunted with air guns and lurchers for forty years and writes regularly for Airgun Shooter and The Countryman's Weekly about hunting and field-craft. In the past he has written for Airgunner, Sporting Rifle, Shooting Times and The Smallholder. He is also a keen wildlife and landscape photographer. Many of Ian's wildlife images can be seen on his Wildscribbler photo website: http://www.wildscribbler.co.uk

As well as many hundreds of magazine articles, Ian has several published books to his credit including:

Airgun Fieldcraft: The Definitive Hunters Guide (Self Published)
The Airgun Hunter's Year (Merlin Unwin)
The Hunter's Way (Self published)
The Hunter's Hound (Self published)
Jaguar! (a hunting novel) (Self published)
Grey Squirrel Control With An Air Rifle (Self published)
Hobby Writing, How To Make Your Play, Pay (Self published)
Through The Wild Eye (Self published)

Ian also writes a regular countryside blog on his website. The site also details how to purchase his books: http://www.wildscribbler.com

Printed in Great Britain
by Amazon